LOST SKI AREAS

—— of ——

Colorado's Central & Southern Mountains

CARYN & PETER BODDIE

THE
History
PRESS

Published by The History Press
Charleston, SC
www.historypress.net

First published 2015

Manufactured in the United States

ISBN 978.1.62619.713.8

Library of Congress Control Number: 2015940375

Notice: The information in this book is true and complete to the best of our knowledge. It is offered without guarantee on the part of the authors or The History Press. The authors and The History Press disclaim all liability in connection with the use of this book.

For the fun of skiing, for the people of skiing, for the sport of skiing, praise God.

Contents

Foreword, by Robert McDaniel   7
Acknowledgements   11
Introduction   13

1. Summit County: Fun in More Ways than One   27
2. Lake County: Mining by Day, Skiing by Night   39
3. Eagle County: Good Times and Skiing Soldiers   44
4. Pitkin County: Ski Area Dreams Turned Sideways   52
5. Garfield County: Riding Up the Big Red Mountain   60
6. Rio Blanco County: Sagebrush Hills for Skiing   66
7. Mesa County: Big Snowfalls, Great Scenery   68
8. Delta County: A Little Fun on the Mesa and Elsewhere   72
9. Montrose County: Tow on a Little Round Hill   75
10. Gunnison County: White Stuff and Western State   77
11. Saguache County: Unique Ride Up a Special Hill   105
12. Custer County: Glass Half Full for the Folks   108
13. Huerfano County: Skiing for Families—On Again,
    Off Again   114
14. Las Animas County: Family Hill at the State Line   120
15. Rio Grande County: Racing Down a Town Hill   124
16. Mineral County: Mining, Ski Clubs and Snow   126
17. San Juan County: Skiing High, Wild and Fast   131
18. La Plata County: Tough Guys, Rope Tows and Local Hills   142

CONTENTS

19. Montezuma County: Two Hills, Two Ski Clubs 149
20. San Miguel County: Skiing Everywhere and a
    Portable Rope Tow 155
21. Ouray County: Skiing Miners, Danger and Disappointment 162

Notes 167
Bibliography 175
Index 183
About the Authors 191

Foreword

I got my first pair of skis for Christmas in 1961, and it was a gift that changed my life. Fifty-plus years hence, the sport of skiing has come to define me as a person like few other things do.

In the early 1960s in southwest Colorado, we had mostly ski hills rather than ski areas. The nearest chairlifts were mountain ranges away. Surface lifts—mostly rope tows and T-bars—were the only lifts used at places like Hesperus, Stoner, Kendall Mountain, Wolf Creek and Durango's local hill, Third Avenue (now Chapman Hill). Wooden skis, lace-up leather boots and cable bindings were the order of the day. My first set of skis, boots, bindings and poles probably cost my dad about twenty dollars.

The popularity of recreational skiing exploded in the 1960s, and we unknowingly rode the wave. Many of Colorado's major resorts were founded in the '60s, including our own local ski area, Purgatory, in 1965. Purgatory's development wasn't only a quantum change in our ski experience—it transformed Durango's economy by making tourism a year-round endeavor.

Skiers of my generation, the baby boomers, came of age during what I think of as the golden age of skiing—all or most of the '60s, '70s and '80s. Fueled by the baby boomers, recreational skiing remained a growth sport throughout most of that period.

While Colorado's skiing roots date back to the Euro-American settlement of the state in the 1860s and 1870s, serious recreational Alpine skiing began in the 1930s, when the first ski tows were built by local ski clubs and other

Robert McDaniel's official membership card for the Durango Ski Club. *Courtesy Robert McDaniel.*

groups of enthusiasts. The 1932 Winter Olympics in Lake Placid and the 1936 Winter Games in Garmisch, where Alpine ski races were first held, captured Americans' attention. The first rope tows in North America (Shawbridge in Quebec and Gilbert's Hill in Vermont in 1934) were soon followed by the first rope tows in Colorado. Local skiers with some mechanical ability modified car and truck engines to power rope tows, and they organized local ski clubs to raise money for gas and other expenses to keep the tows operating.

Colorado's mountain towns were suffering economically in the 1930s partly because of a declining mining industry and struggling farm and ranch operations. They promoted skiing and ski competitions in the hopes of generating some business. The efforts of local enthusiasts and ski clubs in the 1930s, '40s and '50s laid the groundwork for the boom that was to follow. People quickly learned that skiing was fun, even if they were using relatively primitive equipment, everyday clothing and improvised tows. Momentum built slowly during those Depression years, and then World War II put a damper on the sport. Even during those difficult times, however, people found a way to keep skiing.

After the war, skiing rapidly gained in popularity as a winter pastime. Ski areas popped up all across the country, from Vermont to California and Minnesota to Alabama. The best skiing, however, was in the West, and

Colorado was on track to become the number-one state for recreational skiing. Colorado's dominant position was due, in no small part, to the efforts of its early ski pioneers before, during and after World War II.

Looking back after nearly forty years spent in dual careers as both a historian and a professional ski patrolman, the importance of those pioneering efforts to the growth and identity of places such as Aspen, Breckenridge, Crested Butte, Telluride and Durango comes into sharper focus. In this book, you'll learn about the predecessors of Colorado's major resorts—local ski hills from Porcupine Gulch on the west side of Loveland Pass to places like Cowboy Hill only a few miles north of the New Mexico border.

I was lucky to have experienced the flavor of that pioneering period of lift-served skiing, even if it was toward the end of that era. Fortunately, too, there are still people living who remember using those first tows and can tell us about them. Caryn and Peter Boddie have captured some of those memories along with important information about times and places in our skiing history now almost lost to memory.

Robert McDaniel, Durango, Colorado
March 2015

Acknowledgements

We are very grateful to those who passed ski culture on to us, especially our parents, and we thank everyone who shared knowledge, memories, resources and photos with us. Special thanks go to Fred Brewer, Brad Chamberlin, Robert McDaniel, Duane Vandenbusche and Senior Mahoney. Also, a special thank-you goes to Western State Colorado University for sharing former students' theses. Again, thank you all very much.

Introduction

Skiing resembles life. You start at the bottom and work your way up. Along the way you see many pretty scenes and some dim ones. You think at times you will just never make it. But there at last is the top. After taking off your climbers you have that long ride to repay your efforts.
—letter to Bud Davey, 1940[1]

This book is for you. It's the second leg of a lighthearted ski tour of the lost ski areas of Colorado. We hope reading this book will be like gliding through champagne powder on your best skis or snowboard. Enjoy!

Our first book took readers to the Front Range and northern mountains. Also, it gave them a primer on the geography and snow in Colorado, and it told the story of the immigrants who brought ski culture to the state. This book will take you to the central and southern mountains and western plateaus. It will also inform you about a few things related to lost areas that we didn't cover in the first book: the National Ski Patrol, the Tenth Mountain Division and the lost Olympics.

Colorado is a great ski state with great powder. Its different regions are part of that whole and have always been alike in some ways; for example, all over the state, skiing started with folks using Norwegian snowshoes (long wooden skis) to get around in winter and then to race straight down the hill. Also, skiing began as an individual activity but quickly became community fun. In both areas, businesspeople, government workers, teachers and others joined in early skiing and made contributions to the sport and the hills.

Above: Loggers, along with miners and tradesmen, first brought ski culture to Colorado. *USFS photo.*

Left: A woman makes tracks on Norwegian snowshoes. *Courtesy of Summit County Historical Society.*

Summit County ladies pose for a photo. Agnes Finding is fourth from the left. *Courtesy of Summit County Historical Society.*

Other commonalities were that hardworking, humble people skied in Colorado first and introduced skiing to others; ski clubs drove the fun and the sport and did lots of the work on hills and areas; and children and women skied and competed alongside the men from the beginning.

The regions differed in that skiers in the north were loggers and ranchers, while in the southern and central mountains, they were miners and ranchers. Also, people had winter carnivals early on in the north, while competitions sprang up between individual towns and their ski clubs first in central and southern Colorado.

Skiing developed along parallel tracks in different parts of the state: Nordic skiing across flat terrain or straight downhill gave way to a ski-jumping craze, which gave way to skiing with turns, or Alpine skiing. What people used to ski and wore to ski was very different than it is today. Attorney Reese Miller of Durango tells the story of what folks used in the 1950s:

The skis I remember were all wood. Northland was the leading brand with Anderson and Thompson next. Toward the end of the 1950's…a few others started using early models of Head skis.

Bindings were not release bindings! Most were bear trap pieces with a cable around the back of the heel. The hotter skiers—racers—used "long thongs." These were actually long leather straps that tied, by means of a tricky pattern, the boot down with the toe in the bear traps. There was no movement and definitely no chance of release. Buddy Werner, an Olympic downhiller, was a victim of these long thongs with a resulting spiral fracture.

Clothing was non-breathable, non-stretch, and non-comfortable. Later in the decade a few examples of "stretch pants" began to show up. Mostly it was wool sweaters and blue jeans. "Ski gloves" were usually mittens. I

Girls have fun while relaxing at the ski lodge. *Caryn Boddie collection.*

*don't remember many sun glasses, though large yellow goggles were popular.
I don't remember any sun screen until See and Ski in the 60's.*[2]

Ski venues developed to fit the different types of skiing. Folks created single hills and jumps on ranches, runs at the edges of towns and formal resorts with many runs and lifts. There were tiny mom and pop outfits as well as areas with many investors. The history of some of these places is settled and well documented; for others, it's still sketchy, being discovered and written. Some forgotten places are just being remembered.

We hope to give you our best understanding of the lost hills and areas, how they got there and why they went away. We've tried to bring you the facts and figures, along with the human stories, and have organized this book by county, roughly in a big S shape, starting with Summit County and ending with Ouray County, because that made sense to us.

Sometimes, we were not able to identify a specific location because the old descriptions were vague or the evidence has been obliterated by time or development. We let you know when that was the case. Please forgive us if we miss the mark on a hill or area.

Crested Butte Ski Club member Bobby Greenfield races down the slalom course. *Courtesy Crested Butte Mountain Heritage Museum.*

Agnes and Tony Finding enjoy an outing on their Norwegian snowshoes. *Courtesy of Summit County Historical Society.*

At the beginning of each chapter, you'll stand at the top of the run and get a look at the terrain. Next, you'll drop in and ski the runs one at a time, reading about the discrete history and the unique people of each area. Endnotes will direct you to sources that may give you more detailed information.

We give a general location for each hill or area and then—when possible, as some are totally obscured now—give you a more specific location with longitude and latitude (GPS coordinates) so you can go there online, if not in person (please assume that the lost ski areas are on private property unless we tell you otherwise). The locations we provide generally coincide with a point near the base of the ski area or some other point where we could identify a run or lift line from old aerial photographs or maps.

As you read, imagine communities having fun on the hills and how much work it took to make that fun back in the day. The adults did it mainly for the kids, to entertain them in the long winter months and to give them

Many skiers from the Denver Metro Area rented equipment at Eskimo Ski Shops, an ad for which appeared in *Colorful Colorado* magazine. *Caryn Boddie collection.*

something to do. These folks helped both young, talented skiers and a skiing industry bloom and thrive, making the home folks proud. The whole thing snowballed, gaining momentum, and the efforts paid off in economic benefits for the communities and the state.

People were determined to get up the hills. At first, they walked or skied up or had horses pull them up in sleighs. Then, they rode up in buses, trucks or cars—some even drove a car down the railroad track both ways. They created tows from what they had on hand; what they could borrow, barter for or lease from their neighbors; or what some would donate to the cause—rope for tows, gas or electricity and the engines that used them.

World War II shut down skiing and competition on most hills, except for a few close to towns. After the war, some reopened and some didn't. A newswire service told the story. "Skiing will dominate the American Outdoor sports scene this winter as most of the famous ski areas of the West and Middlewest resume operation for the first time since Pearl Harbor."[3]

Alpine skiing had schussed into skiers' hearts before the war, along with European culture, and it continued its rise afterward. Demands for bigger areas with newer lifts and gondolas arose, and the smaller areas had to try to compete with them. Businesses sprang up to sell equipment and clothing to skiers. "Downhill skiing spread from Denver to surrounding ski clubs and more isolated mountains throughout the state. Although each group adopted the trappings of resort culture to differing degrees, they all responded to the influence of European experts," writes professor Annie Gilbert Coleman.[4]

As more people skied, the U.S. Forest Service (USFS) took on a greater and greater role in helping people develop and manage areas and tows (see our first book).

The small ski venues would thrive for a while and then shut down for various reasons, but a few kept going. In Colorado, we see that persistence in active community hills today. Visit them for an old-time skiing experience you won't find at today's big resorts. The following are community hills that are still operating and their locations:

- Chapman Hill, Durango
- Hesperus Ski Area, Durango
- Kendall Mountain, Silverton
- Lee's Ski Slope, Ouray
- Lake City Ski Hill, Lake City
- Cranor Hill, Gunnison

The Colorado State Patrol has served skiers by keeping them safe on the roads to the ski areas. This is one of the snow vehicles they used. *USFS photo.*

In our first book, we categorized the ski venues people created into hills, areas and resorts, depending on size and presence of lifts and amenities, with the help of Bill Fetcher, an expert on lost areas. We also addressed why areas shut down. Basically, it happened for the following reasons:

- competition from larger areas
- loss of customer base and volunteer help
- deteriorating equipment
- inconsistent snowfall
- insurance and regulatory requirements
- financial difficulties[5]

Of course, some hills and areas were lost for a combination of these reasons. Many have been missed and are remembered fondly and some had really sad endings.

NATIONAL SKI PATROL AT LOST AREAS

Skiers expose themselves to risk in order to reap the rewards of skiing. The degree of risk varies according to the type and extremity of skiing we want to do. Logically, as the danger increases, fewer and fewer skiers want to accept the risk entailed until the ones who are left are the extreme skiers who will risk it all for rides or runs in a dangerous areas.

In the old days, skiers looked out for one another, and there seems to have been an ethic where advanced skiers looked out for the safety of the novices, even mentoring them. More than once, skiers with eagle eyes saved people who were using rope tows. Miller had a close call at Cascade near Durango.

A broken leg was a possibility for this young woman at Goldsworthy Lake in 1937. *Courtesy of Senior Mahoney.*

"This was the spot where, but for Dick Yeager, I would have been a fatality in the bull wheel there."[6]

Even so, there were accidents, even tragedies, beginning with Nordic skiing and ski jumping. Families have had to bear the costs of injury and the terrible loss when a loved one was killed. Other people have had less tragic experiences that left them shaken nevertheless.

Also, when Alpine skiing became popular and organized ski areas opened up, more and more people came to ski in the same places. They were of varying levels of ability, and while some were risk takers, others were not; snowplowers and straight-down-the-hill skiers skied the same hills and sometimes ran into one another.

In 1938, Charles "Minnie" Minot Dole, who fractured an ankle while skiing in New England, had a bad experience and was inspired to do

This cartoon from the 1956 *National Ski Patrol Manual* shows how to use a rope tow. *Caryn Boddie collection.*

1. Climb at side of trail. 2. Skiers coming downhill have right-of-way.
Look before you cross a trail. 3. Fill in your sitzmarks, they cause many accidents.

This cartoon from the 1956 *National Ski Patrol Manual* illustrates ski safety. *Caryn Boddie collection.*

something to help others. A manual for members of the National Ski Patrol tells the story:

> *For an hour he fretted in the freezing snow, unable to move without torturing himself, while a friend, Frank Edson, went for help. Two and a half hours later he reached the doctor after a ride down the slope on a piece of corrugated tin without the benefit of a splint on his broken ankle. Later, while still encased in a cast, he received word that Edson had died in a similar accident. Finally, up and around again, he was determined to find a way to prevent skiing accidents and provide care if they did occur.*[7]

The thirty-six-year-old New York insurance broker set up the structure of the patrol first. He appointed seven divisional chairmen, thirty section chiefs and ninety-four patrol leaders. He also set up a liaison with the American Red Cross. Then the organization created rules, requirements for membership and regulations and appointed sixty-four national patrolmen and a national medical committee. One member, Livingston Longfellow, created badges for local and national patrol members. All this took place in the first two years.

From that point on, the National Ski Patrol grew with volunteers and paid staff and with specific purposes and principles to make skiing safer—and it was rewarding to be a ski patroller.

TENTH MOUNTAIN DIVISION

When World War II came along, Dole got another bright idea, which actually grew out of his work on the National Ski Patrol system. He wanted to have a division of the army that would be trained just for mountain warfare. He and other leaders in skiing presented the idea to the War Department, which

A sign at the site of Camp Hale summarizes the ski history of the Tenth Mountain Division. *Courtesy of Bill Fetcher.*

didn't accept it until just before the attack on Pearl Harbor. The Eighty-seventh Infantry Regiment was formed with the Tenth Mountain Division. Dole and his friends set about recruiting soldiers from the ranks of the National Ski Patrol because they were experienced skiers.

Later, recruits had to learn to ski, and they did that first at the division's camp between Red Cliff and Leadville: Camp Hale. Then they would move on for further training at Cooper Hill, which is still operating as Ski Cooper. They also skied on local hills in mountain communities.

After the war, members of the Tenth Mountain Division came back to Colorado and played an essential part in further developing skiing in the state. In particular, they made the big resorts happen, especially Vail. Some of the members ran smaller areas, such as Hidden Valley. A sign in front of the B Hill, the practice hill at Camp Hale, which was created by the division, the National Forest Foundation and others, tells a little more.

LOST OLYMPIC GAMES

In addition to having many lost areas, Colorado has a lost Winter Olympics in its history.

The International Olympic Committee (IOC) awarded the 1976 Winter Olympic Games to Denver in May 1970. Many were thrilled, at least until the logistics and cost of hosting the games started to dawn on Coloradoans, who would have to pay the lion's share. The Colorado Ski and Snowboard Museum at Vail spelled out some problems that arose:

- The U.S. Environmental Protection Act was passed in 1969 and established measures that had to be met on public lands.
- Proposed Olympic venues kept changing: Mount Sniktau did not meet the downhill standards, and negotiations began with Vail to develop Beaver Creek for events.
- A logistical nightmare arose for transportation because both Steamboat Springs and Beaver Creek were over one hundred miles away.
- Funding became a crucial concern as costs rose dramatically.[8]

In 1972, Colorado voters turned down the games. Eventually, they were held in Innsbruck, Austria.

1

Summit County

Fun in More Ways than One

We can have no strawberry, peach, or water melon day; we have no county fair; what would be more appropriate than turning our snow banks to some account other than swelling the streams below us?
—Summit County Journal, *1917*[9]

Summit skiing started with miners using the long boards to get around and get things done, such as Eyvind Flood, who was famous for his skiing prowess. It then moved on to the extreme sport of the day—ski jumping—and then to Alpine skiing, which locals were slow to embrace.

Mail carriers, along with their family members, were among the first skiers in the county. Some contracted with the government to do the job long term, and others stepped up to do it on a moment's notice. Among them was the famous reverend John L. "Father" Dyer, a Methodist preacher.

By the 1910s and early 1920s, Summit County residents had jumped on board with the ski-jumping craze that was hot in many places in Colorado. As was the case elsewhere, the passion for jumping and Nordic skiing was initially fueled by a few individuals who had emigrated from Norway, such as Peter Prestrud, who created jumping hills in his spare time.

Locals jumped at Dillon and used other hills, including one in Breckenridge. The *Summit County Journal* wrote, "The ski course on Shock hill has been put in fine shape and many of the ski enthusiasts have already taken advantage of the last heavy fall of snow."[10] In 1909, an article in the newspaper introduced the sport of "ski-riding" to its readers quite early:

Girls had fun in the early years on Norwegian snowshoes in Colorado. It was common to use only one pole. *Courtesy Animas Museum.*

Great ski jumpers competed at Dillon and across Colorado. *Front, left to right*: Eyvind Flood and Peter Prestrud. *Rear, left to right*: Hans Hanson, Carl Howelsen, Anders Haugen and Lars Haugen. *Courtesy of Summit County Historical Society.*

A ski rider sails at the jumping hill on the lower Blue River, known as Slate Creek. *Courtesy of Summit County Historical Society.*

Norwegian ski-riding, or ski-jumping, as it is popularly termed in America, is a manly and healthful sport which, in the northwest at least, has come to stay. The ski[s] in this country are usually made of birch, ash, or hickory, as pine or soft wood ski[s] prove very expensive articles; they break easily and may be the cause of serious accidents. Birch makes a very good ski, possibly the best for ladies, as it is lighter than the wood used by the professional rider, namely, hickory. The white ash is used mostly by boys, as it is more durable than birch and less expensive than hickory. The jumping ski…should be as long as the height of the man plus the distance he can reach with extended arms overhead, usually 7½ to 8½ feet. The ski[s] for distance traveling are usually longer. They weigh from seven to eight pounds each, a heavier ski being rather better for jumping.[11]

Others came in to join Summit County residents in jumping contests, including Carl Howelsen, Lars Haugen and Anders Haugen. Anders was the standout jumper at the Dillon jumping hill. He "surprised Dillon old timers when he traveled all the way to Colorado during an American sojourn

Anders Haugen skied over the Loveland Pass trail to reach Summit County and would have seen this view on the east side as he skied back home. *Courtesy Woody Smith, Colorado Mountain Club archives.*

and scrambled over the difficult Loveland Pass trail to appear in Summit County. His goal: To attempt a little-known ski jump rumored to be located at Dillon."[12]

Alpine skiing came to Summit County after the 1930s with the creation of a few hills with rope tows. However, the county didn't really get on board until after World War II when the Tenth Mountain Division veterans returned from Europe and lit a fire under everyone with the opening of Arapahoe Basin. "With ski enthusiasm spreading across the nation, Summit County, blessed with ski terrain unrivaled in the country, plodded along, devoting its time to shopkeeping, ranching and small business," wrote Mary Ellen Gilliland.[13]

Breckenridge wasn't alone; folks in other small mining towns were slow to see the economic opportunity recreational skiing represented. People over toward Hoosier Pass and near Climax (formerly in Summit County) took up Alpine skiing first.

Peak 1

In 1910, Peter Prestrud immigrated to Frisco, where his father became postmaster. He is said to have created a ski jump at the south end of town. Though the name indicates it was on Peak 1, the jump was most likely located on the lower flank of Royal Mountain, which looms over town at the end of the Tenmile Range.

Prestrud was young and energetic; on occasion, he would ski to Hot Sulphur Springs by way of Ute Pass to compete and then ski back to Frisco.

Ski jumping apparently took place on and off for many years at Frisco, and a 1969 aerial photograph clearly indicates two parallel jumping hills located near the trailhead at the south end of Second Avenue (GPS coordinates 39°34'6"N, 106°5'58"W). According to coloradoskihistory.com, from 1967 to 1979, high school students trained on the hill, and it was used for training for Junior Olympians in 1989.

Prestrud Jump

By 1919, Peter Prestrud had created a jumping hill at Dillon. It was located above the old town but is today perhaps the only lost ski area in Colorado that is now under water, having been covered, along with the town, by the waters of the Dillon Reservoir in 1963. The authors' best estimate of the location is based on a 1954 aerial photograph and places the top of the jumping hill next to the Dillon Dam Road south of the reservoir spillway tube (GPS coordinates 39°36'49"N, 106°3'52"W).

Eventually, in 1954, the jump was named for Prestrud, but it may have been called Haugen's Hill at first. There's a good reason for that: Anders Haugen set a world record on the hill in 1919 when he sailed 213 feet. A year later, folks gathered to watch him attempt another record-breaking jump. Fans were not disappointed; Haugen rode his skis down the same hill and set a new world record by flying 214 feet.

This was just the beginning of the story for Haugen. John Hafnor tells the best part:

> *The strange story begins in Chamonix, France, site of the first Winter Olympics. The year is 1924. The U.S. team is captained by Coloradoan Anders Haugen...The official results placed [him] in fourth place. Haugen's best jump had actually been three feet better than the best effort*

Right: A big crowd came to watch the ski jumping on the Dillon Hill on March 5, 1923. *Courtesy of Summit County Historical Society.*

Opposite: World champion and Olympic ski jumper Anders Haugen beams after one of his world record–setting jumps at Dillon. *Courtesy of Summit County Historical Society.*

of gold medalist Jakob Thams, but Haugen was marked down for his unorthodox style of leaning forward over his skis…Fifty years later, a Norwegian sports historian stumbled upon an apparent scoring error. To his amazement, the scores didn't add up! Upon further checking, the Norwegian Olympic Committee confirmed that the American was rightful owner of the bronze medal.[14]

The committee invited Haugen to Oslo, Norway, in 1974, when he was eighty-six years old. He went up and received his medal—fifty years late—from Anne Marie Magnussen, who had agreed that her father's medal should be turned over to Haugen.

As of 2015, Haugen was still the only American to win an Olympic medal in ski jumping.

During the Dillon ski jump's heyday, the newspaper ran the headline "Why the Dillon Ski Course Is Rated the Best in the World" atop an interesting story. It read:

> *This week an inquiry was made of professional skiers practicing at Dillon and of Summit [C]ounty ski enthusiasts just why it is considered the Dillon ski course is the best in the world, and why it is expected that a world record will again be made here. Three reasons were given:*
>
> *First—That the contour of the course was such as to allow a jumper to maintain his balance better than any other course; he being able to keep on his feet at a terrific speed while approaching, on and upon leaving the takeoff.*
>
> *Second—Because, and this the [principal] reason, at an altitude of over 9,000 feet a greater speed could be attained and a greater distance beyond the takeoff could be made because of less resistance in the rarified atmosphere. "There is more speed to this course than would dare be taken," said one professional jumper.*
>
> *Third—That the course is covered with "crystal snow," which gave less resistance to the skis and enabled the jumper to have better control preceding the jump.*[15]

SHOCK HILL

Hills for sliding in the county appear to have been moved around, but there were a few primary ones where ski riders competed against one another in the extreme sport of the day. In the early 1920s, the Breckenridge hill was located about a half mile northwest of the center of town (the best estimate of the location is GPS coordinates 39°29'11"N, 106°3'4"W). Shock Hill was found when "Eyvind Flood was casting about for a location on the hill for a desirable slide, and finally laid out a course beginning about 300 feet north of the present course, with a take-off to be erected at the old Pence Miller ditch."[16]

The *Summit County Journal* reported the goings-on of the skiers in Breckenridge, who had formed a ski club and were eager to draw the big jumpers from other hills, especially the hill in Dillon. The article read:

The first amateur contest of the Breckenridge Ski Association will be held on its new course off the lower end of Shock Hill tomorrow afternoon. The course has been put in first-order condition, and the event tomorrow is sure to show up some fine talent that has recently developed in Breckenridge...The young boys only need encouragement and expect a large crowd of spectators.[17]

The paper reported on an event the following year:

A week ago Sunday a number of Breckenridge ski fans pulled off an amateur tournament on the local course on Shock Hill. A large number of spectators were present, and the course was in tip-top shape. Only two jumpers were present, they being Walter Bader and Leo Miller, and Bader carried off the honors with a jump of 110-100-103, while Miller was a close second with jumps of 100-106-108. The course was exceptionally good, and the boys made perfect jumps.[18]

SLATE CREEK COURSE

This jumping hill was located at Slate Creek on the lower Blue River. The authors found no information on the specific location, but a likely spot is one of the open slopes southwest of the community (GPS coordinates 39°46'43"N, 106°10'3"W). Not much else is known about it, except that the best jumpers in Colorado were competing there, and they had audiences who came to watch them. The *Summit County Journal* reported:

Ski jumping is getting to be the order of the day in the sport line in the lower Blue vicinity. Jumping is indulged in every Sunday at the ski slide at Slate Creek, and interest in the sport has become so great that every Sunday a large number of the "ski folks" come to watch the jumpers.

On Sunday, January 23, the young fellows officially organized a local ski club and elected officers to promote the sport. The club is to be known as the Slate Creek Ski [C]lub...A big tournament and contest is to be held at the slide on Sunday, January 30, at which time several prizes will be awarded.

On Lincoln's birthday, February 12, the club will give a big dance at the Slate Creek school house to raise the money for prizes to be awarded at a later tournament, which will be held about the middle of February.[19]

Porcupine Gulch

This area had one run with a vertical drop of one hundred feet and was located along U.S. Highway 6 between Keystone and Arapahoe Basin, on the west side of Loveland Pass. Although the name suggests it was at Porcupine Gulch (near the runaway truck ramp), the authors' review of old aerial photographs indicates that it may have been located about three-quarters of a mile down the road (GPS coordinates 39°37'14"N, 105°55'28"W). It was open only from 1938 to 1940 and had one portable rope tow. Possibly World War II ended its use with the advent of gas rationing and all available men and women devoting their time to the war effort. According to coloradoskihistory.com, "The area was dubbed by locals as 'The Little Sweden Freezer Company' due to the extreme weather found on the pass. The tow engine now resides in the Colorado Ski [and Snowboard] Museum in Vail."[20]

Hoosier Pass

Colorado Wonderland listed Hoosier Pass in 1951 as a skiing center of Colorado. "Located north side of Hoosier Pass, Arapaho Nat'l Forest. ELEV.: 11,000 to 11,500 ft. Season: Nov. 15 to Apr. 1. VIA: State 9 from Fairplay, 13 mi.; from Breckenridge, 10 mi. RUNS: One, 600 ft., one 800 ft. TOWS: None."[21] Other sources say that it had a rope tow at this time, but the tow had stopped working.

The two ski runs, though almost grown in, are still visible from the highway below the switchbacks on the north side of the pass (GPS coordinates 39°22'16"N, 106°3'26"W), and an old log warming hut is still standing next to the road.

It had been open for over a decade during the time when downhill skiing was new and growing in popularity in Colorado. The Summit Historical Society tells the story:

> *Imagine this: a perfect site for a ski area is found on Jan. 27, 1938. On Feb. 6, 11 days later, 150 people, including Count Phillippe De Pret of Belgium, ski instructor at the Broadmoor Hotel in Colorado Springs, are skiing there. Sound impossible? It's true! The ski area was located on the north slope of [Hoosier Ridge].*
>
> *This "sports mecca" was the project of the South Park Lions Club. The club hired Bill Bergren of Alma to "make it all happen—quickly." In*

Hoosier Pass had an electric tow. *USFS photo.*

1934, the building of Hoosier Pass Road split the Bemrose Placer into two unequal parts. Bergren utilized structures on the bigger (east) section—two large buildings and a few cabins (one of them this 500-sq.-ft. log cabin with a semi-convex, asphalt-covered roof)—in the ski area project.

By January 1939, the site boasted a restaurant (a large room with booths and tables, a bar, a dance floor and a "rock-ola with records installed"), rest rooms, a warming hut/drying room (most likely this cabin), cabins for lodging, a storehouse and a glassed-in observatory that was connected to a two-story boardinghouse. The latter had a porch and a spiral staircase. The site also sported a bobsled course, three ski runs, a ski jump and a Chevy truck engine-powered 800-ft. tow line.[22]

It's also easy to imagine that this was one of the places to be for locals and people who drove up from Colorado Springs, just as Berthoud Pass was the place to be for many from Denver. Folks came as much to see and be seen as to ski. It was a more sophisticated brand of skiing and socializing than the one the Norwegian miners had brought to the county.

It was unusual for a ski area to operate during the years of World War II, but Hoosier Pass did through the 1940s. "The sports area stayed open until

Good times were found at Hoosier Pass. *Courtesy of Summit County Historical Society.*

at least 1949, but skiers had to hike to the tops of the remaining two runs and small jump, carrying their skis, because the tow line didn't work."[23]

BRECKENRIDGE BALL PARK

This town hill was created by locals for local kids at Carter Park on the east side of town (GPS coordinates 39°28'39"N, 106°2'23"W). According to coloradoskihistory.com, it was open for ten years (1976–86) and had a 760-foot-long rope tow and a hill with a vertical drop of only 202 feet. "This ski hill was a local town place to learn to ski. A rope tow was installed in 1976 but a decade later the rope was stolen. The area asked for a variance from rope spiraling regulations with no luck. It never opened for the 1986–'87 season."[24]

2

Lake County

Mining by Day, Skiing by Night

We rode in an old military ambulance from our school in Climax to the hill...I
also used the ski jump that was built to the left of the mountain. It scared the hell
out of me.
—Max G. [25]

This county has a rich mining history. It has famous residents, including
Margaret and J.J. Brown of "Unsinkable Molly Brown" fame. It has
renown because the Tenth Mountain Division skied and trained nearby in
Eagle County. A memorial to the division stands today at the entrance to
Ski Cooper.

What is not as well known is that community ski hills informed the men
in the Tenth Mountain Division who would later found large ski areas in the
state. Annie Gilbert Coleman writes, "The practice of skiing recreationally
on the weekends introduced the division's cohort of skiers to the community-
oriented ski areas...Colorado ski areas that stayed open during the war and
were accessible from Camp Hale found themselves inundated by them on
the weekends."[26]

There had been skiing in Leadville before the Tenth Mountain Division
arrived in the county. The *Estes Park Trail* told about it:

Leadville—The organization of a ski club to operate all during Leadville's
long winter and make this city a second St. Moritz, at a meeting just
held here proved the sentiment is in favor of organization of a large club.

Leadville has from four to five months of real winter weather during which skiing is fine and there are many places where elegant courses can be made and some fine leaping grounds provided.[27]

CLIMAX

This ski area was located on Chalk Mountain (GPS coordinates 39°22'13"N, 106°11'28"W). The *Manual of Colorado Skiing* for the 1957–58 ski season—about twenty-five years after locals started skiing there—described its attributes:

Located 99 miles from Denver on Colorado Highway 91 atop 11,320 ft. Fremont [P]ass. A 2800 ft. T-Bar lift with a capacity of 600 skiers per hour operates from 10 a.m. to 4 p.m. on Saturday and Sunday with night skiing on lighted slopes Wednesday and Friday from 7 p.m. to 10 p.m. Downhill runs ½ mile long with ¼ mile of all runs open slopes above timberline. Vertical drop of 1,500 ft. One racing trail and one 80 ft. jump. Practice slope for beginners. Operation from November 15 thru April 15 including Thanksgiving Day and Christmas Week except Christmas Day. Warming house, Ski Patrol First Aid room and ski equipment rental shop. Fremont Trading Post adjacent to parking area offers Ski Shop, general store, food market, service station and garage with excellent restaurant facilities open Saturdays and Sundays.[28]

The manual for the 1958–59 season said there was a new warming house, serving light lunches.

These logistics only begin to tell the story about Climax—named by railroad people who were thrilled that they successfully laid track to that high elevation—an area beloved by the men who mined molybdenum at Climax Mine, and their families.

"Up we went and down we came," said Joan Brookshire, who learned to ski at the area and grew up in the town of Climax near the mine. "On top you could see all over. It was a beautiful experience."[29] She added that they'd go skiing if it was a blizzard or if it was thirty below and that the area was a fantastic babysitter with Ski Patrol on duty; kids would walk over from the town and ski all day, take their lunches and go home at four o'clock.

In the years she skied there, kids in school got free lessons and may have gotten free passes. In December 1947, the *Steamboat Pilot* wrote about this development:

Ski meets were common at Climax. *Courtesy of Joan Brookshire.*

*Norman Richardson and Bernard Herbert will open the Continental Ski
[S]chool at Climax, Colo., on Dec. 31. In addition to conducting the
school, the two men will coach the Continental Ski club junior and senior
teams. Herbert and Richardson both are veterans of the 10th Mountain
[D]ivision and have had wide experience in teaching in eastern resorts as
well as competing in many races.*[30]

A tower at the top of the Climax tow was well built by Climax Mine workers. *Courtesy of Joan Brookshire.*

As the Climax children grew up, they worked at the ski area. "As we became older we became loaders. Some of us were ticket takers."[31] Brookshire worked in both capacities and mentioned having frostbite on her fingers a few times.

She said there was a rope tow—one of the first in the state—in 1938 and that after 1940, when she was about twelve years old, Climax decided to buy a T-bar lift for employees. She remembered going with her father to other ski areas to investigate different types of lifts, including T-bars and chair lifts.

Her dad, James Kauffman, was a mechanic working at Climax and was put in charge of the lift. He and other men built steel towers from the base to the top. "All the guys who worked on the project worked at Climax," she said.[32] They installed huge floodlights and made night skiing, the first in the state. Plus, there was a great big parking lot that Climax or the Colorado Department of Transportation (CDOT) plowed out.

The ski area provided a great time for many for years, and the Continental Ski Club connected with other clubs in the state. The club hosted many meets and competitions, including a state championship and a "De Molay" meet.

The Climax Molybdenum Company closed the town in 1962, and it soon disappeared due to the expansion of the mining facilities and tailings. The ski area was lost as folks relocated to Leadville or other towns and probably skied at Ski Cooper and Dutch Henry and then went on to the resorts that were opening.

Dutch Henry

This is a hill in Leadville at the southwest corner of town near the Colorado Mountain College campus (GPS coordinates 39°14'18"N, 106°18'14"W). According to coloradoskihistory.com, the Cloud City Ski Club ran the area, which had a rope tow, a warming hut, night skiing and snowmaking. Remnants of the tow are still visible. The hill was small, with only a two-hundred-foot vertical, but it was near to where people lived. Today, it is a private tubing hill for club members and is also used for training by the college ski area management program.

Dutch Henry provided a lot of fun for the people of Leadville. *Peter Boddie collection.*

3
Eagle County
Good Times and Skiing Soldiers

When winter months set in on the community, winter sports for Eagle and neighboring communities will include a ski course and lift thanks to the plugging away of a handful of local men.
—Eagle Valley Enterprise, 1948[33]

It took an outside catalyst, but once the town of Eagle got onto the idea of skiing, residents worked together to make two hills and keep them going. At the heart of it all was community.

In another part of the county, a hill in a temporary community provided training for soldiers: the B Hill at the Tenth Mountain Division town known as Camp Hale. There, soldiers who didn't know how to ski learned before they joined the ranks of troops sent to Europe during World War II.

A couple other ski hills sprang up, too. Reportedly, one of the big resorts gobbled one up and shut it down. Another along Interstate 70 near Avon became part of Beaver Creek.

WHITTAKER RANCH

Gordon and LaVeta Whittaker owned a ranch of about two thousand acres on Bruce Creek to the southeast of the town of Eagle. It had hills that townspeople used for sledding and sliding on toboggans. In 1938, one of the

LaVeta and Gordon Whittaker pose at their ranch on Bruce Creek with the ski hill behind them.
Courtesy of the Eagle County Historical Society and Eagle Valley Library.

hills became the focus of a larger effort involving skiing (GPS coordinates 39°34'43"N, 106°44'3"W), according to the local newspaper:

> *Some twenty five or thirty outdoor sportsmen have recently formed the Eagle Valley Winter Sports Club, for the purpose of promoting winter sports throughout the valley...The club has prepared a ski course on Whittaker [Hill] seven miles southeast of Eagle on which much work has been done this winter, but which will be greatly improved next summer, especially by building a good jump and a [toboggan] slide...Those promoting the club hope to be able to hold winter sports carnivals and competitive ski runs, when the course has been made suitable.*[34]

World War II came along and curtailed plans, though folks did ski on the hill some, just walking up and skiing down.

In 1948, plans to improve the hill began again, and a tow was constructed. The *Eagle Valley Enterprise* gave a good picture of how this happened:

Next Sunday will see the completion of a 1,200-foot lift on Whittaker Hill and Bruce [C]reek, just off the Brush [C]reek [R]oad which was started in August and has been the scene of feverish activity on every Sunday since August 29, when the first post hole was dug…while a number of people entered into the picture, actually the work is the product of the labor and push of a few local men who have sweated out the installation of the tow for the past six Sundays and hope to make next Sunday the day of completion.[35]

Rancher Gordon Whittaker made his contribution by signing a contract that allowed the community access to "40 acres of his ranch to use as a ski area."[36]

In 2011, Kathy Heicher was president of the Eagle County Historical Society, and she wrote about Whittaker and the local ski history. Her work was published in the newspaper, and further quotations in this section are from it, except where noted otherwise. She wrote, "Credit the determination of community leaders to provide a recreation opportunity for local residents, the generosity of a Bruce Creek rancher and the ingenuity of several Eagle citizens for making that downvalley ski opportunity happen." Donations for the tow from community members included poles, money and more. Heicher continued:

Fred Downey, who operated the Texaco station, donated the motor and chassis of a car bought at a sheriff's sale as the power source for the tow. Skip (Melvin) Chambers, 70, who skied Whittaker [H]ill as a kid, remembers specifically that the "power plant" was a 1938 Ford one-ton truck with a V8 engine.

The area was open on weekends and holidays. As many as fifty skiers would come to play, using hiking boots and old skis with bear-trap bindings. They had been handed down from the skiing soldiers at Camp Hale. The rope tow—like rope tows throughout Colorado—was a challenge to use because it was always twisting. "Big gloves were a must. Leather work gloves were preferred. The savviest skiers soaked the palms of the gloves with beeswax to toughen the leather to help grab the rope." The Whittaker family added a ski shack to the hill by 1952, with a warming stove, benches and counters. LaVeta Whittaker made pots of chili for the skiers, with the help of Eileen and Florence Randall.

Mick Randall added a special contraption as a feature of the hill: a "ski bike" without brakes.

Folks ride the Whittaker Ranch tow in 1951 and have fun on the hill. *Courtesy of Eagle County Historical Society and Eagle Valley Library.*

Randall, an inventive guy who worked hard to help make the ski facility a reality, hit upon the idea of extending an old bike frame and bolting a couple of sawed-off skis onto the contraption in place of wheels...Skip Chambers took the ski bike for a memorable, out-of-control run down from the top of the ski hill.

"It looked to me like it would be an easy thing to ride," Chambers... remembers, with a somewhat defensive laugh. He hit a hole at the bottom, and destroyed the ski-bike in a horrific crash.

The Whittaker ski hill came to an end when townsfolk decided to move the ski tow closer to town, where it would be more accessible to local kids.

EAGLE SKI HILL

Eagle residents installed the rope tow at the top of Sixth Street on the Cole Black ranch above the cemetery near the town water tank (GPS coordinates 39°39'3"N, 106°49'25"W) in 1954. The local Lions Club, led by Glen Chambers, spearheaded the project. Chambers added a safety feature to the tow: a gate that would shut it off in an emergency. Sure enough, someone got his scarf caught in the tow. Just before he was choked, the tow tripped the safety rope and shut off.

This new ski hill proved to be a great playground for local kids. The *Eagle Valley Enterprise* reported:

> Local kids flocked to the little two-run slope. On winter afternoons, as soon as school let out, Chambers and his friends would run to his dad's gas plant, grab a five-gallon can of gas, then head out to fuel the tow and do some skiing.
>
> The ski runs, while short, were steep. Just hanging on to the rope tow was a challenge.
>
> "You had to be tough to make it to the top because of that last rutted hump," remembers Bill Johnson.
>
> The kids crafted a ski jump by sawing the back legs off of a picnic table, positioning it against the hill and covering it with snow.
>
> "You could catch some air off of that thing," Johnson recalls. Skiers could rest on benches installed where the ski run flattened out at the bottom.

The Eagle Ski Area kind of faded away as the years went on and other attractions, such as a new high school in Gypsum, took kids elsewhere. There may have been years when snow was scarce, as well. There had been good times on "Cemetery Hill," as the area was sometimes called, but they were over by the 1960s.

MEADOW MOUNTAIN

This ski hill sprang up for the 1966–67 ski season after Vail had opened to the east. Its base was where the Holy Cross Ranger District office is along U.S. Highway 24, south of Interstate 70 at the Minturn exit (GPS coordinates 39°36'21"N, 106°26'45"W).

According to coloradoskihistory.com, the area had a Poma lift and a double chairlift "built by Telecar with a length of 2250', 571' vertical, 840 passengers per hour (pph) capacity, with a speed of 500 feet per minute (fpm)."[37] It also had the only luge run in Colorado.

The area was listed as a new area in the ski information manual put out by the Colorado Visitors Bureau in 1967:

> Wide open meadow skiing, excess of 110 acres of skiable terrain... Season November 25 to May 1. Area served by one double chairlift and one pomalift [sic]. Total uphill capacity of 1,200 skiers per hour. Beginning and practice area. Six runs with the longest 7,700 feet, shortest 500 feet, vertical drop of 900 feet. Slopes maintained by tracked vehicles. Ski Patrol. Ambulance at area.[38]

Author Peter Bronski tells current skiers how to backcountry ski the meadows today in *Powder Ghost Towns*. He also gives an account of what took down the area. The year the ski area opened was reported as "encouraging but not spectacular" by the *Denver Post*. The very difficult second season kept skiers away for the third season. The area tried to rebrand itself as a learning ski hill and offered deals to elementary teachers and students: $10 season passes for teachers and $15 season passes for students in Eagle County and Lake County. Vail purchased Meadow Mountain for $3 million, in spite of opposition from residents of Minturn, and then promptly shut it down at the end of the 1969–70 season.

> Some people say it was because Vail didn't like the competition. Others argue, convincingly, that Vail was thinking about participating in the bid for the 1976 winter Olympics, and Meadow Mountain was a potential venue. Eventually, Vail also purchased the "Nottingham property" west of Meadow Mountain in 1971, and built Beaver Creek instead (it was approved in 1975). Also in 1971, The Forest Service successfully negotiated to buy the Meadow Mountain/Oleson property.[39]

Visitors to the ranger district can see the hills of Meadow Mountain behind the buildings. Also, the base lodge is visible from Interstate 70.

B HILL, CAMP HALE

The Tenth Mountain Division of the U.S. Army's Eighty-seventh Mountain Infantry Regiment was formed in 1941 by the War Department. This was

A Tenth Mountain Division trooper is caught in mid-air with a rifle on his back, circa
1942–44. *Courtesy of Eagle County Historical Society and Eagle Valley Library.*

just before the attack on Pearl Harbor. They made their camp in Eagle
County, between Red Cliff and Leadville, complete with streets and two
newspapers to report on what was happening. The first recruits were skiers.
Subsequently, the B Hill, or B-Slope, was developed to train recruits who
had never skied before (GPS Coordinates 39°25'8"N, 106°18'47"W). Bill
Fetcher, of Steamboat Springs, tells the story:

> *Once the supply of recruits who could ski had dried up the Army had to
> train never-evers. This was the apparent purpose of B-Slope* [B Hill],
> *which takes its name from its location at the south end of Camp Hale's
> B Street just past the Camp Hale Memorial Campground. After showing
> some promise as skiers on B-Slope they'd be bused up to Cooper Hill (Ski
> Cooper) for further training. (The name B-Slope is also used on the Camp
> Hale interpretive signs along U.S. 24 and has a certain Army charm to it,
> given the military's obsession with initials, acronyms and abbreviations.)*
>
> *I've been told that during Camp Hale's final years of operation B-Slope
> was operated by Special Services, which sees to the recreational needs of
> armed forces members and their families; selling event tickets, operating
> movie theaters, bowling alleys, restaurants and the occasional ski area.*

*Meanwhile, Cooper Hill had been turned over to the City of Leadville.
Camp Hale was deactivated in 1965.*[40]

The *Camp Hale Ski-Zette* ran a column by Sergeant William Wolf on what
it was like to train as a recruit:

*Keep your elbows in, bend your knees more, keep your hands lower. You
heard those words so frequently during the first week of skiing, it became
an obsession with you. While skiing this past week you didn't hear quite as
much yelling as the fellows were getting accustomed to their skis.*[41]

4

Pitkin County

Ski Area Dreams Turned Sideways

*So ends a decade of Montezuma Basin's history that at times has been as
confusing as a soap opera on television.*
—Paul Hauk, 1978[42]

In the 1880s, silver brought the first boom to Ashcroft, about ten miles
south of Aspen on Castle Creek. Shortly thereafter, the town boasted
some 2,500 residents, a couple of newspapers, a school, two sawmills
and twenty saloons. It's possible that Ashcroft residents got around on
Norwegian snowshoes in the winter. Then, the mines played out, the
town went bust and residents left. By 1900, only two people remained at
Ashcroft. Eventually, the land was deeded to the U.S. Forest Service.

Another boom came nearly forty years later: recreational skiing and
tourism. At first, the prospectors for the new economic engine thought
skiing would grow in the Little Annie Basin and at Ashcroft, but the dream
turned sideways on them, and the lode they were seeking emerged in
another place: Aspen. What most people don't know is that the prospecting
these guys did helped to make Aspen successful.

Years later, others had fresh ideas about where skiing should take place:
Montezuma Basin at the head of Castle Creek and Redstone in the
Crystal River Valley. Also, Aspen residents skied Independence Pass, even
holding slalom races there.

Summer skiers use the rope tow at Montezuma Basin. *Courtesy of Mary Eshbaugh Hayes.*

LITTLE ANNIE

It all began in 1936. Tom Flynn had grown up in Aspen, and his father ran the Top Lift Mine in the Little Annie Basin. He attended a party in California where he happened to have a conversation with a guy named Billy Fiske. They talked about building a ski area in America that would be similar to St. Moritz, Switzerland.

Flynn must have said his Aspen was the place. He brought Fiske and other potential investors to Aspen to explore the opportunities: Ted Ryan, son of the Warren Buffet of the 1920s; Robert Rowan of a Los Angeles real estate family; and Thor Groswold, the great skier and ski manufacturer.

They went to the top of the Little Annie Basin (approximate GPS coordinates 39°7'54"N, 106°49'31"W), guided by the Willoughby boys. Years later, another Willoughby told the story in the *Aspen Times*:

> *Fiske was immediately convinced of Little Annie's potential. Like anyone who has ever looked down the basin and across the valley to Hayden Peak, Fiske found his St. Moritz in America. He proceeded to the Forest Service office to examine land titles and snow records.*[43]

Soon Fiske and Groswold brought back a ski expert, Otto Schniebs, to tour the basin with them on a tractor and sled and test snow depth and quality. It was good enough for them. Flynn, Fiske, Ryan and Rowan formed the Highland Bavarian Corporation.

The men were gung-ho and pushed to open the ski slope the next winter. Tom Flynn became the project manager, and he supervised the construction of a lodge and headquarters while living at the Hotel Jerome in Aspen. The slope opened at Christmas with a big party for the people of the town.

Pals stand in the doorway at the Highland Bavarian Lodge. The images above them were hand painted. *Courtesy Aspen Historical Society.*

The group bought and built on the property that had been the Tagert ranch. It was located just above where Conundrum Creek splits off Castle Creek, at the site of the old mining town of Highland. The Highland Bavarian Lodge, which remains, had two bunkrooms, a dining room and a living room and a large, double-sided fireplace built of red sandstone.

The group spread word of the venture coast to coast to reach investors. Robert Benchley, a famed humorist for the *New Yorker*, created a brochure about it that was distributed widely. Through their efforts, the partners made many people aware of Aspen and the great country surrounding it. According to Willoughby:

> *The goal for 1937 was to promote the fledgling ski resort by enticing skiers and potential investors from both coasts...Billy Tagert hauled guests from the lodge to the bottom of Little Annie in his horse-drawn sleigh for 50 cents a ride. From there they could ski back toward the lodge along a trail cut by Ted Ryan in the fall. That trail emptied into a meadow at the side of the valley, and that became a beginners area. That meadow was the location of Aspen's first ski races.*
>
> *Hardier skiers could attach skins to their skis to climb the basin to the top of Richmond Hill. From there, they could either ski down the basin or cross over the basin divide to Buckhorn, then ski through Tourtelotte Park and down mining roads to Aspen.*[44]

Two more big names in skiing, Andre Roch and Dr. Gunther Langes, came to inspect the Little Annie Basin. An article published after Roch's death tells the story:

> *"In 1936...Roch imagined a vast alpine complex that would include a Zermatt-style alpine village and Swiss tram rising 4,000 vertical feet to the timberline bowls on Hayden Peak," wrote Peter Shelton in the book, Aspen Skiing, the First Fifty Years.*
>
> *"He was convinced that Aspen Mountain, directly above the town of Aspen, could be superior to anything in the U.S. at that time, but that nearby Ashcroft, 'once developed, would be a resort without any competition.'"*
>
> *Roch had been hired to give ski lessons that winter to guests of the Highland Bavarian Lodge and to Aspen locals...Roch also convinced local skiers that they should cut a run on Aspen Mountain to draw attention to the skiing potential in Aspen. He laid out the narrow winding trail, and in the summer of 1937 local volunteers cut the trees and named it Roch*

Run... The trail ended up being 6,600 feet long, about 50 feet wide, and dropped 2,550 vertical feet. And it helped put Aspen on the skiing map.[45]

So, despite creating a run on Aspen Mountain, Roch still recommended that the big ski resort be built at Ashcroft with ski runs from the top of Electric Peak. The Highland Bavarian Corporation adopted his recommendations, purchased Ashcroft and got ready to make the area happen. Willoughby continued:

When America entered the war, however, all efforts ceased. Ted Ryan, who had sustained a serious skiing injury, offered Ashcroft to the 10th Mountain Division with a dollar-a-year lease. Some early 10th Mountain activities were headquartered there. Billy Fiske joined the Royal Air Force and was the first American pilot to lose his life when his plane was shot down. The aging Tom Flynn returned to his farm in California.[46]

After the war, Ryan was the only partner left. He saw that skiing was going to be on Aspen Mountain rather than at Ashcroft, but he didn't give up on the dream for decades. Eventually, he settled for a ski touring operation at the lodge location and deeded the land at Ashcroft back to the U.S. Forest Service.

MONTEZUMA BASIN

Montezuma Basin is perhaps unique among the lost ski areas in that it was only operated in the summer because it was so high and inaccessible; it could only be reached by jeep road after the snow had melted along the lower slopes. In fact, its purpose was to be a summer training area for ski racers and students after the regular ski season had ended.

The area was located near the end of the Castle Creek Valley, past the Montezuma Mine and at an elevation of thirteen thousand feet in a north-facing basin below Castle and Conundrum Peaks, where snow lingered well past midsummer (GPS coordinates 39°1'1"N, 106°51'29"W). A portable rope tow was used to haul skiers up the main slope, but many also walked up to ski various areas in the upper bowls high above timberline.

Folks enjoy a summer ski in Montezuma Basin. *Courtesy of Mary Eshbaugh Hayes.*

Author and photographer Mary Eshbaugh Hayes, a longtime resident of
Aspen, talked with the authors about skiing at this area. She said that Rick
Rosen of Aspen and Taos ran the rope tow as part of a summer camp for
college students in the late '60s.

Hayes was doing freelance photography for an article for *SkiMagazine*
then and got a ride up to Montezuma Basin via the jeep road. She said, "It
was so scary, I walked the whole way back down."[47]

A 1978 chronology written by Paul Hauk, retired White River National
Forest Recreation and Lands staff officer, told the story of an area that
changed hands numerous times:

*This "on again, off again" summer-use area at an elevation of 13,000'
in the basin on the north side of Castle Peak southwest of Ashcroft finally
reached the special use permit preliminaries in January, 1966. When
Max Marolt of Aspen, and Dick Milstein of Glenwood Springs, contacted
me...Max, a well-known local ski racer and brother of C.U. ski coach Bill
Marolt, wanted to install a portable ski tow, extend the Montezuma Mine
road approximately one-half mile to the base area where a small parking
lot and shelter-toilet facility would be constructed on part of two mining
patents.*[48]

The report shows in detail the work the U.S. Forest Service did with and
for private citizens on the small ski area near Aspen and details the number
of people who were brought into the issue, including a mayor and senator.
At one point, someone wanted to build a chairlift at the remote location.

For the USFS, working with ski people was sometimes like herding cats; on
the flip side, the USFS permitting and safety regulations were burdensome
to the visionary ski people. Eventually, both gave up.

The USFS did not allow the tow to operate during 1977 and '78. Lift-
served skiing at Montezuma Basin was at an end.

REDSTONE

This area was built at the town of Redstone, near the mansion built by John
Osgood, also called the Redstone Castle (GPS coordinates 39°10'26"N,
107°14'28"W).

According to coloradoskihistory.com, Frank Kistler proposed the
Redstone area in 1956 and hired a number of people to do different studies,
including Dick Durrance and Willy Schaeffler. They formed a group called
the Redstone Development Company and considered two hills behind the
Redstone property.

They contacted the U.S. Forest Service and made application for a permit
because they would need more than the private land to have enough vertical
drop and trail length. The U.S. Forest Service denied their application for
a ski area permit because the area was "submarginal" in terms of snowfall.

The group decided to build a small area on the private land with one
beginner slope. They installed a short Roebling T-bar lift near the area
opened on Christmas Day 1960 and ran off and on through March 1961,

Machinery for the tow at the Redstone Ski Area has its own beauty. *Caryn Boddie collection.*

when it closed for good. The "submarginal snowfall" apparently proved true, and the limited slope sometimes required "using your poles in spots to get back to the bottom," as one local put it.

The T-bar and one building are still in place but can only be seen by accessing the private road to the Redstone Castle, which you can do if you pay to take a tour of the beautiful and historic castle.

5

Garfield County

Riding Up the Big Red Mountain

When more men from the Glenwood [Civilian Conservation Corps] *camp are available they will continue work of clearing the run on Red Mountain, where skiing may be enjoyed this winter.*
—Glenwood Post, *1939*[49]

Skiers may know this county only as that place down valley of Aspen or that area west of the big resorts on the way to Grand Junction, but this county hosted ski areas years before Aspen became well known for skiing.

Residents of Glenwood Springs got fired up about skiing before World War II and created places to ski on that big red mountain you see west of town. Hardy residents, who just wanted to have a little fun, created ski areas the locals enjoyed for years. They did so with enthusiasm, contributing everything from blood, sweat and tears to acres of land.

One area, called Holiday Hill, operated from 1948 to 1951 at the base of the current Sunlight Mountain. Reportedly, it had a rope tow powered by a Buick engine, and the tow was the second longest in the state and went eight miles per hour. Sunlight Mountain Resort and Ski Area was still operating in the county when this book went to print, perhaps carrying on the legacy of family- and community-friendly areas that characterized the first Garfield County ski areas.

LOOKOUT MOUNTAIN

The first ski area at Glenwood Springs seems to have been on Lookout Mountain located on the east side of town. There is little information about it, but an item in the *Steamboat Pilot* on November 10, 1938, read, "The new ski course on Lookout mountain [in] the Glenwood area is being constructed."[50] Another article, this one about Red Mountain skiing, mentioned the ski course on Lookout Mountain the year before.

Apparently, the Lookout Mountain ski hill only operated for a short time before interest shifted to the west side of town with the construction of a new area on Red Mountain. The authors were unable to pinpoint the location of the ski run on Lookout Mountain.

RED MOUNTAIN

Glenwood Springs chose a site for a ski area on Red Mountain in the late 1930s (GPS coordinates 39°32'39"N, 107°20'13"W). It was close to Glenwood Springs and accessible for its residents. One newspaper reporter wrote in 1940, "The Red Mountain ski course can be easily reached by walking or driving across the Roaring Fork River bridge…A large number of skiers were on the course Sunday and most of them climbed to the top of the run, which is affording great sport to those taking the opportunity to use it."[51]

Like many small-town areas, the Red Mountain course was built when community members pitched in to make it happen. They counted on the physical labor of community members and workers in the Civilian Conservation Corps (CCC) camp in Glenwood Springs. A local, J.E. Sayre, donated the land for the area during a meeting of the city council. George Sumers volunteered his tractor for construction of the course. The *Glenwood Post* was there to cover it all from the beginning. "During the past few weeks groups of men have been working on the ski run, clearing it of small timber and underbrush. Future and fur[ther] development at the site will be accomplished by the city, the national parks service, and the CCC camps of this locality."[52] Later, the *Post* reported that the run was about one and a half miles long and could be extended up and down the mountain and had locations "for every type of skiing."[53]

In January 1940, the Burlington Railroad declared that Glenwood Springs was one of the four great areas for skiing in the west, and people stopped off by train to ski Red Mountain.

Skiers enjoy a day on Red Mountain. *Courtesy Frontier Historical Museum.*

The ski hill was deemed worthy of further development, even a chairlift. Writer Willa Soncarty told the story of its construction in a look back in her column "Time and Again" for the newspaper. She wrote, "The CCC, under National Park Service supervision then began the construction of the wooden lift towers and terminals. Engineering and survey services were provided free of charge by Les Finley, Bud Ayers, and Leo Fick."[54]

People were invited to ride the chair to the top of the ski course to enjoy a barbecue put on by the chamber of commerce of Glenwood Springs. The *Post* reported:

> *The ski tow, an aerial and chair type, has been under construction for about a year. During the summer the tow was tested and conditioned and several of the towers were strengthened with concrete bases. Forty people can be taken up the tow at one time and 220 can be transported up the mountainside every hour. On the 26th, the tow will start operating in the morning and go throughout the day, thus allowing rides for everyone.*

A woman rides the Red Mountain chairlift. *Courtesy Frontier Historical Museum.*

> *Passengers will be loaded at the depot at the lower end and unloaded at the upper end. The tow is about 5,000 feet long, one of the longest in the west.*[55]

Snowfall wasn't all that great for the hill, though, and there were other problems. Soncarty described it:

> *Testing continued throughout 1941, but an accident, which severely injured one man and toppled a tower, closed the lift to use until January, 1942. Limited use and World War II threatened the closure of the course, but with aid of the Chamber of Commerce the area would open to weekend use again in 1943.*[56]

Red Mountain operated through 1947, but there were further safety issues with the wooden towers, and it was tough for volunteers to keep up with the fast-growing oak brush on the runs. It closed for two years.

Then, members of the community stepped forward again to keep the thing going: a group of eight businessmen got aggressive with the brush and cleared the runs, and a financial backer named Jess Barnes gave the necessary funding. These folks operated the area for two seasons, 1949–50 and 1950–51. Soncarty continued:

> City Council in 1951 awarded the ski area lease to Joe Juhan. As part of the lease, Juhan was required to replace the 15 wooden towers with 18 steel towers. He widened and improved the trails. He also improved the shelter at the top of the tow.[57]

The new steel towers were painted bright orange. Staff was hired: Bill McClure—a former ski instructor at Winter Park—ran the lift. Ed Jones—formerly a ski instructor at Camp Hale, Winter Park and Steamboat Springs—became the ski instructor for the area. Glenwood Ski Club members became ski patrolmen.

Lift tickets were $2.50 per day, and a season pass was $32.50. Soncarty wrote:

> Weather and progress, however, sealed the fate of the Red Mountain Ski Area. Snowfalls in the years following the 1951 opening [were] poor and limited. Competition from newer and more modern areas drew local skiers away. The summer operation of the lift proved to be beneficial, but the winter operations proved economically unsound. Joe Juhan was released from the ski area lease at the end of the 1958–59 season.[58]

Several towers are still standing in place on Red Mountain. You can see some of them if you hike the winding three-mile switchback road to the top (not open to public auto access). You will be rewarded with the same striking views skiers must have had.

GLENWOOD MOUNTAIN PARK

Still, there were community members in Glenwood Springs who couldn't let the ski area die. The person who owned land at the top of Red Mountain, Margaret "Cap" Smith, tried to revive skiing on the mountain one last time. In 1963, she and other Glenwood residents decided to move the lift up higher, figuring snow conditions would be better up there, and created

Glenwood Mountain Park (GPS coordinates 39°31'55"N, 107°20'32"W). Soncarty wrote:

> *They purchased a 900-foot-long Hall double chair lift, constructing a six tower lift. The lift opened the summer of 1965 and operated the 1965–66 season as the Glenwood Mountain Park. The poor road to the area as well as the lackluster skiing forced the venture to close after just one season. The short lift would later be sold to the ski area at Sunlight.*[59]

A *White Book of Skiing* listed the area:

> *Glenwood Mountain Park is an entirely new skiing area three and [a] half miles west of the city of Glenwood Springs, to be operated by Glenwood Lift, Inc., W.E. Kirkendall, general manager, PO Box 987, Glenwood Springs, 81601, phone 945-6206. The new chairlift is expected to carry 1,000 skiers an hour to the three runs, and a second lift is planned for construction next summer. There will be a ski patrol, ski school and snack bar at the area. Plans are for another restaurant on the "Rim" in a season or two, to take advantage of the view of the Colorado and Roaring Fork River valleys. The new area will be accessible to all Glenwood Springs facilities…lodging, eating places, swimming pool, stores, entertainment and transportation. Glenwood Springs is on Interstate Highway 70, U.S. Highway 6, 168 miles from Denver and 88 miles from Grand Junction.*[60]

Glenwood Mountain Park lasted only a short time, but perhaps the community became closer and stronger for having built it and run it, not to mention the fun everyone had on Red Mountain, first lower down and then up top.

6

Rio Blanco County

Sagebrush Hills for Skiing

*The Meeker-Rifle Road is drying up fast, but there are twelve or more miles on
top where snow is drifted so badly that sleds are necessary.*
—Steamboat Pilot, 1925[61]

Ranchers and other residents in this county were usually busy with cattle,
drilling for oil and the county fair. The census also had to be taken. It was
a tough job in many Colorado counties; Rio Blanco was no exception. Before
recreational skiing emerged here, one woman used snowshoes to do her job
as an "enumerator."[62] Later, residents built a ski jump on Nine Mile Hill.[63] In
between, Rifle residents got together to ski. The *Steamboat Pilot* reported:

> *A ski club has been formed at Rifle with 35 members attending the first
> meeting. Gaylord Henry is president of the club and it is planned to develop
> a ski course on the Claude Rees ranch north of town.*[64]

REES SKI RANCH

It was reported that the course, which was located north of town fifteen miles
at Rio Blanco Hill, was inaugurated in 1949. "The Rifle Ski club had the
official opening of its course on the Rees ranch north of town on December
24," said the *Pilot*.[65]

Coloradoskihistory.com reported more detail on the Rees Ski Ranch, including that the hill had one 1,600-foot rope tow and a small cabin for a warming hut.

> *The area was founded by local skiers from the Union Carbide's uranium-vanadium mill in Rifle and the Bureau of Mines Oil Shale Demonstration Plant. Engineers from the companies constructed the gas-powered tow. The tow had three emergency stop stations; one at the top, middle and bottom. The area mostly operated on weekends and charged a dollar per day. The funds paid for gas and tow repairs. The area's staff consisted of volunteers that ran the ski patrol, maintained the slopes and tow, and kept the fire in the hut going. The school system also ran a bus to the ski area on Saturdays. Rees Ski Ranch began to lose popularity in the 1950's when other ski areas opened near Glenwood Springs. The area closed in 1953.*[66]

The authors were not able to pinpoint the location of the Rees Ski Ranch. However, based on the length of the rope tow, the logical location for it is a spot just over the line into Rio Blanco County—a small drainage facing northeast near the top of Rio Blanco Hill, the low highway divide between Rifle and Meeker (GPS coordinates 39°42'18"N, 107°56'26"W). There is a line through the trees and oak brush up to a ridge but not much evidence of ski runs.

7

Mesa County

Big Snowfalls, Great Scenery

Three young men of Clifton, Colo., spent a week on the Grand Mesa in Mesa county, trekking across country 15 miles on their skis to a shelter house.
—Steamboat Pilot, *1937*[67]

Mesa County is the fourth-largest county in Colorado, boasting high mesas, desert canyons, broad valleys and big rivers. It's known for the Colorado National Monument, the city of Grand Junction and its peaches and wineries. Also, it has great skiing atop Grand Mesa, where Powderhorn Ski Area is still operating.

At least three lost ski areas existed on the mesa years ago, on the west side below Lands End, near the top at Mesa Lakes and on the north side at Mesa Creek. Before they came to be, folks skied up to the mesa from the towns below it, and it seems that winter carnivals were held there in the 1920s. The *Aspen Daily Times* reported on one before the fact:

> *Ski enthusiasts [of] three towns, Grand Junction, Delta and Cedaredge are stirred to a high pitch of interest with the announcement that the annual Grand Mesa Ski Carnival will be held on February 8th.*
>
> *Fully a hundred or more novices and expert ski riders of both sexes and all ages are expected to join in the excursion [to Grand] Mesa. A caravan of ski fans will leave Delta the morning of February 8 and pick up fellow sportsmen along the way, all to proceed to the top by sleigh.*

Tobogganing and ski jumping will feature [in] *the tournament which will last several days.*[68]

Articles in the *Steamboat Pilot* referred to the Mesa Nature and Sports Club in 1931, which apparently not only took advantage of snow on Grand Mesa but also ranged far and wide, including outings to places near Steamboat Springs. Later references to the club call it the Grand Junction Ski Club.

LANDS END

It seems that this area was popular and may have been the location where folks held winter carnivals and ski parties (see Delta County section). Abbot Fay writes, "Delta and Grand Junction skiers would weekend at Land's End on the mesa, a sheer drop into the Gunnison valley below, and tested the north rim, which would eventually emerge as Powderhorn."[69]

The authors couldn't find much history about the operation of the Lands End hill but were able to locate the area using old aerial photographs and a few bits of information. It was about half way up the infamous Lands End Road on a north-facing slope between two switchbacks (GPS coordinates 38°59'38"N, 108°14'39"W). Although nearly grown in now, the ski run appears to have been at least eight hundred feet long and was steep enough to have included a jump.

MESA LAKES

The authors found only limited references to a ski hill at Mesa Lakes on the north side of Grand Mesa. The precise location couldn't be identified, but it was probably near the Mesa Lakes Lodge. Some of the early ski excursions on top and across the mesa likely made use of government cabins here and at other locations on the mesa. Regular skiing at a more formal hill, however, was probably hampered by difficult access in mid-winter, and in 1942, skiing moved down to a lower elevation along the highway at Mesa Creek.

Mesa Creek

This area was located along Colorado Highway 65 on the north side of Grand Mesa (GPS coordinates 39°3'59"N, 108°6'21"W). Coloradoskihistory.com reports that locals know it as the "Old Powderhorn," and it operated for twenty-six years, from 1940 to 1966.

The *Steamboat Pilot* reported on an event that was held there in 1942:

> *Sunday, January 18, was open house at the new ski lodge on the Grand Mesa course, skiing area of the Grand Junction club. Thru* [sic] *cooperation of the forest service the entire area was moved lower down to a more accessible spot and the new lodge built.*[70]

A U.S. Forest Service sign located at the site in 2014 read, "Starting with a rope tow, Mesa Creek eventually included two Poma lifts and an old Civilian Conservation Corps building for a warming hut. An organized ski patrol and ski school were both established and run by locals from Grand Junction and the surrounding region."

The area is listed in more than one issue of the *Manual of Colorado Skiing and Winter Sports*. For the 1957–58 ski season, the listing gives the location as ten miles above the town of Mesa and forty-two miles from Grand Junction. The manual described it:

> *Two rope tows in tandem; lower (beginners) 600 ft. long serves a gentle slope and upper (intermediate) 1,100 ft. long serves a more advanced slope. A Pomalift* [sic], *2,952 ft. long and 865 ft. rise, serves three courses from 3,800 ft. to 5,400 ft. long for intermediate, advanced and expert skiers. Tows operate Saturdays, Sundays and Holidays from 10 a.m. to 4 p.m. Daily tow fees: Club members, Juniors (Hi. Sch. and under) 75¢, Seniors $1.50 and non-members $2.50. Club memberships, Juniors $2, Seniors $3, may be obtained at the ski area. Warming shelter and hot lunch facilities. Ski instruction available. Volunteer ski patrol on duty. Area Manager, Jack Force, Mesa, Colorado.*[71]

The manual for the 1962–63 ski season read, "Area designed with emphasis on fun for the whole family. Lunch facilities available at area."[72]

The Colorado Visitors Bureau put out information on the area in 1966–67 ski season, saying that the Grand Mesa area was a totally new operation:

A member of
the University of
Denver Ski Team
does a freestyle
move. *Courtesy of
University of Denver
Special Collections
and Archives.*

*Runs descend from heavily wooded, table-flat top of 10,000 foot Grand
Mesa, world's largest flat-topped mountain…Protected north slope
and natural bowl assure top snow conditions for normal season from
Thanksgiving to mid-April. One chairlift and two pomalifts [sic] carry
skiers to seven runs with the longest 8,000 feet, shortest 1,300 feet and
a vertical drop of 1,600 feet. Beginning and Practice area. Total uphill
capacity 1,530 skiers per hour. Slopes maintained by tracked vehicles.*[73]

Coloradoskihistory.com says that there was also a volunteer ski patrol
there and that the chairlift was called the Lions Lift. It eventually moved
to Powderhorn.[74]

8
Delta County

A Little Fun on the Mesa and Elsewhere

A group of boys started on skis Monday of last week in an attempt to ski to the top of the Grand Mesa national forest from Cedaredge, Colo. They were forced to turn back before they reached their goal. The boys reported that they had discovered one of the finest ski slides in the country on this trip.
—Steamboat Pilot, *1926*[75]

This county is characterized by orchards, vineyards, cattle drives, murals, sheepdog trials and beautiful landscapes. Its residents have enjoyed skiing as well.

In 1924, the United Press reported out of Delta about a ski party that residents arranged:

> *A party of twenty-five Delta ski fans, together with some invited guests from Grand Junction, plan within a few days to have a week-end party in the way of a ski jaunt over Grand Mesa.*
>
> *The party will travel via bobsled as far as possible up the Alexander Lakes road and from there hike on their horizontal stilts over the 10-foot drifts to various of the hundreds of lakes on top of the mesa, 11,000 feet above sea level.*[76]

There was a community hill at Crawford about which the authors could find little information. Fred Brewer wrote these notes about it: "Mentioned in the history of a ski pioneer (Jack Gorsuch) as one of the first night lighted ski areas in Colorado (fifties?, sixties?). Nothing else is known."[77]

Also, someone told us that there was a hill called Fawn Valley, but we could not find the location on aerial photos. Brewer noted that it was along Highway 133 in the mid-1960s. "We visited the Paonia public library in 1992 and the librarian remembered the area. A friend had skied there. 'Dangerous,' she called it. She called it 'Somerset' which is the name of a small town near Fawn Creek."[78]

If Fawn Valley was close to or past Somerset going east, it would have been located just over the line into Gunnison County.

Author Sandra Scott grew up with the area as part of her life. She wrote, "In my hometown, Paonia, Colorado, just a couple hours outside of Aspen, my father built a ski area called Fawn Valley in partnership with another man. It had rope tows and ran on the weekends. My mom made the chili and the pies for the concession stand…My father trained hundreds of beginner skiers, preparing them for Aspen."[79]

There are two other lost ski areas in Delta County, which once provided a lot of fun for residents. The Cedaredge ski hill was located a few miles north of the town of Cedaredge at the base of the Grand Mesa and operated after World War II. Later on, after the highway was improved to allow winter access to the top of Grand Mesa, a small area called Rimrock opened and operated in conjunction with the Alexander Lake Lodge. There has been some confusion in the past; people listed the areas as one but called it by either name.

CEDAREDGE

The 1951 Christmas issue of *Colorado Wonderland* lists this area as being located along Colorado Highway 65 on the south side of the Grand Mesa outside the national forest boundary. It was four miles from Cedaredge and nineteen miles from Delta. The magazine states that it was at an elevation of seven thousand feet, had one run of nine hundred feet with two rope tows, one four hundred feet and one two hundred feet. The area operated from January 15 to March 15.[80]

Based on this description and a review of old aerial photographs, the authors believe they have found the location for the Cedaredge ski hill along the side of Highway 65 (GPS coordinates 38°57'59"N, 107°56'6"W). During the period of operation, from as early as 1946 and continuing into the 1950s, the old highway was located about a quarter mile to the south, and the ski area probably included part of the meadow located below the current road and a beginners' area with the shorter rope tow.

According to coloradoskihistory.com, the Cedaredge hill had a ski jump in 1946 and operated with tows in the 1950s. It is not known when the area closed, but it was probably gone by the time the highway was moved and improved sometime in the late 1950s or early 1960s. Given the low elevation and southwest-facing slope, the area probably operated somewhat sporadically.

RIMROCK

Rimrock Winter Sports Area was a separate area located high up on Grand Mesa behind the Alexander Lake Lodge.

The "Rimrock" name refers to the nearby Crag Crest cliffs that form the highest part of the Grand Mesa and not the ski hill itself, which was on a pretty gentle slope. The area was operated in conjunction with the lodge by John and Barbara Burritt, from 1967 through 1970. It included one rope tow located along the right side of a meadow cleared of timber, about a quarter mile east of the lodge (GPS coordinates 39°2'36"N, 107°57'39"W). According to Brad Burritt, his grandfather ran the rope tow and his aunt ran the concession stand. He joked that he and his brothers were the informal ski patrol.[81]

Katherine Kawamura told some of the story, writing for the *Grand Junction Daily Sentinel* in 1967:

> *In a scenic setting surrounded by ice covered lakes, the Rimrock Winter Sports [A]rea has been beckoning scores of visitors…The development has been practically a one-man operation. John R. Burritt of Redlands Mesa conceived of the area, then fought red tape, finances, and a timber-covered slope to realize his dreams.*
>
> *Offered this year is a gentle slope for snow bunnies with a rustic, A-frame warming hut. The beginners' slope is served by a 600 foot rope tow.*
>
> *The area, located near Alexander Lake is open daily except Monday. Ski rentals and lunch concession are available…In coming years, Burritt plans development of additional slopes to attract intermediate and advanced skiers. The ridge on which the ski area is located offers a varied terrain and snow conditions, Burritt said.*[82]

9

Montrose County

Tow on a Little Round Hill

A couple of Montrose boys said Sunday that Roch [R]un reminded them of a doctor's prescription. You learn to ride it or break your neck. You know, the kill or the cure way.
—Bud Davey, 1940[83]

Great rivers like the Dolores, the Uncompahgre and the Gunnison define much of the character of this county, alternately forming broad valleys and deep canyons, and the few areas with consistent snow, like the Uncompahgre Plateau, are largely remote and inaccessible in winter. However, residents did manage a little bit of skiing on a round hill near the eastern end of the county during the 1930s.

CERRO SUMMIT

This area was located at Cerro Summit along U.S. Highway 50 east of Montrose on the way to Gunnison (GPS coordinates 38°26'35"N, 107°38'26"W). The short hill and runs are visible to the south of the turnoff and parking area at the top of the pass. During a cultural resource inventory requested by the Colorado State Historic Preservation Society—the Rotary Club was about to build new trails—information about an early ski area there was uncovered. Laurie Brandt wrote about the new find:

Runs are still visible at Cerro Summit in Montrose County. *Caryn Boddie collection.*

Volunteers from the Chipeta Chapter of the Colorado Archaeological Society and Alpine Archaeological Consultants…indicate that a historic rope tow for skiing on the hillside was discovered in the vicinity of the current sledding hill. The rope tow site consists of two horizontally mounted automobile wheels that are 300 feet apart and 80 feet different in elevation. The 21-inch diameter wheels are similar, probably from the same vehicle, and have castellated nuts and steel spokes with faded yellowish paint. They are probably from a 1928 or 1929 Model A Ford and the wheels are mounted on upright buried axles.[84]

10
Gunnison County
White Stuff and Western State

*Five feet of snow. Mail carrier Lawson started to Sargents on snow shoes
yesterday. A little slide off Granite Mountain, just above the Magna Charta
[T]unnel, gave the boys a scare Tuesday.*
—*Tomichi Topics,* White Pine Cone, *1886*[85]

Though beautiful, Gunnison County has never been the easiest place to live in the winter months; it's often frigid with deep snow. That hasn't been a deterrent to living in the county—because of skiing.

The snow and cold have been a very positive draw, according to Dr. Duane Vandenbusche, a professor at Western State Colorado University (WSCU) and ski history expert. Said Vandenbusche, "Of all the places in Colorado, I don't think we take second place to anybody."[86]

In turn, there's no doubt that skiing has added to the happiness and prosperity of people living in Gunnison County. "It's been tremendously important," Vandenbusche said, "the main source of income for a long time and a source of pride for everybody. It brings in revenue, a tremendous amount of publicity, created numerous Olympic skiers. It's been an absolutely crucial part of the history of the Gunnison County."[87]

The whole thing started in the same way it started in so many areas of the state; before the railroad, skis were the only way to get around. J.E. Phillips told the story in a letter he wrote to the *Gunnison News-Champion* in 1940 about the late 1800s:

Miners at Irwin skied to get around and for recreation, competing with other miners. *Courtesy Crested Butte Mountain Heritage Museum.*

We had to learn if we wanted to go anywhere. All outlying districts were inhabited in those days. Irwin, Gothic, Crystal City, Pittsburgh, and all over the Elk Mountain region. If residents wanted to come to the big town, Crested Butte, they had to come on skis or snowshoes, and it was not an uncommon sight to see 50 or more pairs of skis in front of M.J. Gray's store while miners and their wives were inside buying goods.

About 1886 we had a ski club that attracted much attention all over the country. We gave exhibitions on the steep hillside run just south of town. We gave the fastest runners first, second and third prizes of real worth usually gold stick pins made to order. Had folks from Gunnison and other towns such as Montrose, Delta, Grand Junction, Salida and Denver come to the ski exhibitions at the Buttes. There were also snowshoe contests and exhibitions near Gunnison on north slopes but spring snow at the county seat was uncertain.[88]

After the railroad came, skiing changed, as it did in other parts of the state, and folks had access to distant hills, such as Marshall Pass. Still, common folk created ski areas close to home using their ingenuity, resources and muscle so their children could ski nearby. The hills provided a great deal of wintertime fun and made the cold months bearable for any humans not hibernating like bears.

Students started coming to Gunnison 1911 when the liberal arts college opened. They needed something to do during the winter months, and skiing

The WSC Ski Team poses for the 1950 *Curecanti*, a college publication. *Left to right*: Sven Wiik, Thor Groswold, Glenn McLean, Jim Hearn, Don Larsh and Coach Adolph Kuss. *WSCU archives, Leslie J. Savage Library, Western State Colorado University.*

WSC coach Sven Wiik skis at Rozman Hill. *Courtesy Crested Butte Mountain Heritage Museum.*

was it. In fact, after World War II, the sport developed largely because of the efforts of students and faculty. With the prodding of ski enthusiasts, such as Olympian Crosby Perry-Smith, Western State College (WSC) developed a ski program at the college for its team, the Mountaineers. Over the years, this necessitated the creation of ski hills to accommodate ski team training.

The WSCU website tells what the hills did for the college and skiing. "Western has a proud tradition of sending both athletes and coaches to the Olympic Games. In the past century, 22 Mountaineers competed in the Olympics, and three Western graduates went on to coach Olympic teams for the United States."[89]

The following is based largely on the work of Western State students. The authors cite a student thesis at the start of each section below, except for the section on the Marble Ski Area.

CUPOLA HILL

This hill started out as the site of a smelter and then as a town overlook and popular parking spot for young couples. It's located east of the residence halls for what is now WSCU in Gunnison (GPS coordinates 38°33'6"N, 106°55'0"W).

In her thesis, "Zip-N-Walk a Mile: Cupola Hill," Kimberly O'Neill told the hill's story.[90] Henry F. Lake built a road up the hill and then built the cupola atop it—with a 360-degree view of the area—in the 1890s. "It wasn't until the late 1920's or early 1930's that skiing started on Cupola. The hill was open country, close to town and the snow was deep." At first, folks walked up and skied down. Rial Lake, one of the well-known skiers of the county and son of Henry, referred to this as the zip-and-walk-a-mile method of skiing.

In 1933, folks were looking for ski hills, and Cupola Hill had potential. A crude ski course was laid out there, which was open most weekends. O'Neill continued:

> *Skiing in the 1930's wasn't like we think of skiing today. Mrs. Ann Zugelder recalled her experiences there as jumping the irrigation ditch and walking up the hill for a quick run down. "Only the young and ambitious wanted to ski." This limited the number of skiers at Cupola. On weekends, the crowds rarely exceeded*

Cupola Hill was a busy place in the 1950s. *WSCU archives, Leslie J. Savage Library, Western State Colorado University.*

fifteen. It also required the ambition to make your own [skis]. Bill Calkins recounted making [skis] from hickory or ash. He would cut the skis ten to twelve feet long and four inches wide. From there Mr. Calkins and friends took their skis to a Mr. Forbes, better known as "Forbie," who ran the boiler room which was located behind the present-day Taylor Hall. Forbie would place the skis into the steam pipes for a week or so until the wood was moist enough to bend. Calkins would pick up the skis, bend up the tips, then apply bee's wax or paraffin to the bottoms with a hot, flat iron to insure easy gliding.

John Knowles purchased "a pair of Northland skis from Enders Hardware on Main Street…The precious skis cost Knowles twelve dollars and were made of prime hickory." Boots were regular shoes, and bindings were improvised from shoe leather or inner tubes or simple straps that were nailed to the boards.

Julia Jackson and a friend ride the tow on Cupola Hill. *WSCU archives, Leslie J. Savage Library, Western State Colorado University.*

Between 1945 and 1950, WSC built a rope tow on Cupola Hill with a government grant for recreation. Students and faculty worked hard on the project. They used a Buick engine and 1,500 feet of rope, which was war surplus. O'Neill wrote:

> *Sven Wiik was elected to pull the motor up the hill on a toboggan and Adolf Kuss and the maintenance crew put the tow together. After this was completed, they found that having the engine on top of the hill was too dangerous. As the rope went up the hill it twisted and could get tangled up, interfering with the motor. Thus, the motor was soon moved to the bottom of the slope. The tow could only hold four to five people at a time, and someone would keep watch to make sure there weren't more than the specified number of people riding the tow.*

Students and townspeople skied the hill for a number of years and may have returned to ski Cupola during World War II because of the hill's proximity to town. There was night skiing on its slopes in the 1950s. The WSC team used the slope for practice but soon looked for a better hill.

SAGEBRUSH HILL

This hill was located one mile west of Gunnison on the south slope of the Palisades (GPS coordinates 38°32'52"N, 106°57'26"W). In her thesis, "The Sagebrush Hill—Left to the Wind: The Practice Ski Course," Marilyn Strobeck wrote, "The project, called the Gun Club or Practice Ski course, was underway by mid-January of 1939."[91]

It was the Great Depression, and men were being put to work through the Works Progress Administration (WPA). The people of Gunnison—including Rial Lake, Mayor Eddie Grout and others—went to Grand Junction to seek approval for a WPA project that would build a "major ski course" and improve an existing ice-skating rink in Gunnison. "The project was approved in record time calling for $17,000 of WPA funds, to be balanced by $5,000 of local funds. However, these funds could not be secured for the project unless an official group or company was created." The townspeople created the Gunnison County Ski Club, which is also called the Gunnison Valley Ski Club by some or simply the Gunnison Ski Club.

The U.S. Forest Service supervised the building of the course and trucked in men from the WPA to work on the site. The club had to put the men to work immediately or the grant money would be lost. So they got together timber, cable, bull wheel, hand grips and a six-cylinder Buick engine. It may have been the same Buick engine used on Cupola Hill because it was provided by Henry F. Lake Jr. Strobeck told the details of the construction:

> *The laborers were used to put up two wooden terminal blocks. This was accomplished by digging a pit, putting a log in the pit, and filling the pit with rocks around the log. The bull wheel and the Buick engine were located on the top of the hill by the upper tower and of course, the lower tower was at the bottom of the hill. A cable was harnessed around the bull wheel along with a spring load having weights that went up and down, which held the cable tight. Hand grips were put around the cable as a* [means] *for holding on to the cable. The WPA workers also cleared the hill of the brush and rocks, and cleared to 400 feet. The practice course had a 2,000 foot run, with an average grade of 20 percent. The original plans called for lighting the course for night skiing; however, lights were never put up. The area could accommodate 150 to 200 skiers without crowding. Although the winter weather was severe, the Practice Ski Course was completed on April 1, 1939—ready to operate the following winter.*

In the midst of construction, folks discovered that the location of the ski course was not feasible; it was an exposed slope that got too little snow and too much wind. But the Gunnison County Ski Club and the mayor didn't call the construction off; they didn't want to lose the grant money, and they intended to work on other slopes north of the city. The rope tow was never used, but before the hill was left to the wind, locals skied it using the zip-n-walk-a-mile method. Eventually, everybody headed up to Pioneer to ski, abandoning the unique towers the WPA workers had built. They were still there in 2014.

Quick's Hill

Before Pioneer was built near Cement Creek, there was another ski hill in the same area but on the west side of the main East River Valley along the old railroad tracks (approximate GPS coordinates 38°48'32"N, 106°54'3"W). Strobeck wrote about it in her thesis as well.[92] Quick's Hill was used by the WSC Hiking and Outing Club, which was headed by Clarence Rockwell. Strobeck described the struggle to reach the hill:

A little freestyle skiing was fun on Quick's Hill back in the day. *Courtesy Crested Butte Mountain Heritage Museum.*

> *To get to Quick's Hill, a car was driven on the railroad tracks. If a train was coming from Crested Butte, the car had to be run into the snowbank on the side of the track so the train could pass…When evening came, the car was turned around after the train had [passed] and the skiers headed back to Gunnison.* [93]

Abbot Fay wrote that students simply rode the train to the hill:

> *In 1916, Moses Amos Jencks, a business professor at Western State College there, started skiing as a regular sport, with token credit given for the training. Joined by local enthusiasts, students made short runs around the town, but for deeper drifts, they took the narrow-gauge train to Quick's Hill, near Crested Butte, twenty-eight miles north.* [94]

Quick's was another hill where folks walked up to ski down.

White Pine

On the other side of Gunnison County, miners worked to extract gold and silver in the 1880s near the isolated mining camp of White Pine on Tomichi Creek. It was some thirteen miles northeast of Sargents, which is thirty-two miles east of Gunnison. The Silver Panic of 1893 hit in the United States, and White Pine was abandoned until 1901. From 1902 through World War II and into the 1950s, miners came back to mine for other minerals, and there was a small boom.

During the second boom, the mine company, Callahan Lead-Zinc, provided a variety of entertainment and recreation for its people, including a ski hill across the main road from Tomichi Creek, called Whitepine.

According to Vandenbusche, the ski hill was on the southeast side of town right in back of the company's mill. The authors weren't able to pinpoint the exact locations, but the lower ski hill was apparently close to town and the creek (estimated GPS coordinates 38°32'26"N, 106°23'39"W), while the upper location was in a side valley a half mile or more to the east (estimated GPS coordinates 38°32'31"N, 106°22'59"W).

In her thesis, "Whitepine Ski Area: Recreation for Miners," Judith A. Hollingshead wrote of the 1940s, when Pioneer had gotten underway:[95]

> *Whitepine was not to be out done, and they put in their own ski slope. As reported by Mrs. Lola Goolsby in the "Whitepine" column: "Among the equipment brought into Whitepine is an 1,800 foot ski tow used in previous years of another Callahan camp. R.J. Flynn assistant superintendent will be in charge of the skiing when they decide where the course is to be located."*
>
> *The chosen location was across the main road from Tomichi creek, remembered George Means, whose father had helped clear the trail with a tractor. The ski run was ready a few weeks later. Mrs. Goolsby commented that "grown-ups were out Sunday on skis," officially bringing the sport of skiing on designated slopes to the community of Whitepine.*

The mine company had a cat and groomed the slopes—and was lucky to have an experienced skier on hand:

> *Mr. R.J. "Jim" Flynn, the assistant superintendent in charge of the little ski area, had been a champion skier, recalled Anne Steinbeck, a former teacher in White [P]ine. When the area was moved before the 1947–48 ski season "Mr. and Mrs. Flynn went up to our ski course at the Erie above*

the North Star Sunday to try it out" reported Mrs. Goolsby the following November. Flynn taught the residents of the area how to hang onto the tow rope—not an easy task. The tow would pull the skier up a fairly steep slope, a rather jerky endeavor, due to the alternating slackening and tightening of the rope. The engine, run by electricity from the mill could pull several children up the hill at one time. In the Spring, when many people were using the tow and the weather was warm, the rope would get stretched out and would drag in the snow, according to George Means.

People who skied Whitepine remember that the slope was about two hundred feet long, well groomed, wide, great for beginners and had plenty of snow. One of the challenges of the hill was that "the skier had only about 75 feet to either stop or run to avoid landing in the creek—many remember learning to stop in a hurry."

Steinbeck reported that the children had up-to-date equipment because their families were making good money in mining and that they thoroughly enjoyed skiing there. She said the students even taught her how to ski before the second mining boom went bust:

Once again the little community was empty, and the noises of a bustling mining camp gave way to the silence. The skiers no longer covered the hill with their tracks. The rope tow was eventually moved to [Cranor] Hill… Only the memories of those who skied the tiny ski area remain; clear visions of learning to use the rope, then conquering the hill and avoiding the creek, along with friends and family who have long-since joined the realm of "fond memories" or past [acquaintances].

PIONEER

When the Gunnison Ski Club decided it needed a location for a ski hill where there was plenty of snow, it looked north of the city toward Crested Butte. Gary J. Sherman wrote down the story in his thesis, "I Forgot My Parachute: A History of the Pioneer Ski Area."[96]

The site the club found was on Cement Mountain, twenty miles north of Gunnison and two miles east on Cement Creek Road (GPS coordinates 38°49'15"N, 106°51'33"W), where the snow reached the top or third wire on a barbed wire fence most winters. Sherman described the area's beginning:

Left: Skiers line up for the tow at Pioneer. *Courtesy Crested Butte Mountain Heritage Museum.*

Below: An old gear wheel collects aspen leaves at the Pioneer Ski Area site. *Caryn Boddie photo.*

At this point, a new family to the Gunnison County became very important. In the spring of 1938, Art Fordham and his family, living in Aspen, accepted the position of Vice President of the Gunnison Bank & Trust Company. Art's two daughters, Audra and Ann, had reached the ages of eleven and eight. Audra, who was extremely interested in skiing, was very disappointed to learn that her father had taken a job in Gunnison.

In the summer of 1938, the family lived at the Pioneer Resort on Cement Creek. On a horseback ride, the Fordhams discovered that the mountain had slopes to rival those on Ajax Mountain in Aspen. Fordham contacted the ski club about the location. The club consulted the U.S. Forest Service about it and obtained a permit. It would cost them one dollar per year to use.

Members of the ski club went to Gunnison County and its commissioners to get permission to improve roads to the site. The commissioners approved, not realizing how much work it would be to maintain the ski area down the line. At the beginning of 1939, Rial Lake and Chuck Sweitzer, who were officers in the ski club, walked and skied Cement Mountain to find runs to develop in the following spring and summer. They had accomplished their task by May, and the work to clear the slopes began, which involved cutting down trees, removing stumps and rocks and filling in large holes, all without modern equipment and at nine to eleven thousand feet elevation. It was exhausting work.

The Little Dipper at Pioneer was one of three main runs. *Courtesy Crested Butte Mountain Heritage Museum.*

Volunteers—ski club members, businessmen, townspeople and WPA workers—created three runs: an advanced slope, an intermediate slope and a beginner's hill. They also created a downhill course on the lower part of the advanced course. The *Gunnison News-Champion* held a contest to name the slopes for what it called the Gunnison-Pioneer Winter Sports Area. Audrey Miller won the contest and named the advanced course Big Dipper, which was notoriously steep and tough; the intermediate course Little Dipper; and the beginner's slope Milky Way, which would have a three-hundred-foot rope tow with a forty-foot rise in elevation.

It was apparent to the ski club that a rope tow would not do on the more advanced slopes. It looked for alternatives, and what it decided to do became quite an endeavor:

> *Wes McDermott had traveled to various ski areas around the country and had seen what was called a chair lift, powered by a large auxiliary engine. He suggested to the ski club that they try to construct a chair lift. So far none existed in Colorado. To build a chair lift of the size needed to serve the Pioneer slopes would be a monumental task. In fact, not many people really believed the small ski club could do it. The Forest Service and the county commissioners were very skeptical. There was one thing they did not realize, and that was the determination of men like Lake, Sweitzer and McDermott.*

What could they use for their chair lift? Lake suggested a mining tram from the Blistered Horn Mine close to the summit of Cumberland Pass. They managed to purchase it from the Swiss company that owned it for $50 because the president and owner loved skiing. Originally, it had cost $23,000 dollars.

How would they get the tram to Cement Creek, some fifty miles away? They went up to the mine hopeful and were taken aback at the towers for the tram, which were twelve-by-twelve-foot cedar timbers. In Shepard's words, this is what happened:

> *The group worked for about three and a half hours trying to dig up the massive towers without much success when, as in almost true storybook fashion, an old sourdough miner came up to the group from out of the hills to give them the secret of removing the towers. "If you will help me get some dynamite here from out of my cabin, I'll show you how to take down those towers with ease," he said. The old miner placed two sticks of dynamite at the base post of each tower and lit the fuse. The towers came toppling down almost perfectly intact.*

The men loaded the towers on an old four-wheel-drive army truck from World War I that belonged to the county highway department. The timbers were so heavy that several men had to ride on the hood and front bumper of the vehicle to keep the front end on the road.

At the hill, Ronald Hume was in charge of raising the towers for the lift. First, they had to construct a road with a USFS tractor. They drove the towers up and lowered them down to their positions on the mountain by rope and cable.

It was necessary to splice cable to the cable taken from the mine, which is not an easy thing to do. The ski club got Clarence Tombling to do it. He owned a jewelry store at the time but had spliced cable in the mines in his early years. "The finished cable was approximately sixty-one hundred feet in length and was one and one-fourth inches in diameter."

The men strung the cable on the towers with support from shives at each one. On each end of the lift, they placed bull wheels and fitted the cable around them. The one at the bottom of the lift was mounted to a large, four-horsepower Wakishaw engine, which had a six-gear Brownie transmission. Shepard described the final hurdle to develop the lift:

> *The last problem concerning the cable was to achieve the proper tension along the entire route. In order to be able to adjust the slack in the cable, the last tower on the lift was mounted on a moveable platform and was tied to several cables that extended about one hundred feet beyond the tower. The far ends of the cables were fastened to large blocks of cement. The blocks of cement were moved with a block and tackle, thus slightly moving the tower and adjusting the tension on the cable carrying the chairs.*

In 1939, the lift was finished. It was the first chair lift in the state and was 3,000 feet long, rising 1,300 feet in elevation.

However, the U.S. Forest Service didn't like it that skiers would ride along at ten to twelve feet off the ground, so the ski club had to lower the cable. Then, the USFS realized that people caught their skis along the way and were jerked off the tow when it was at a low height, so they made the club raise the cable up again. The club had to prop the cable up with poles that had shives atop them.

The ski club members made the chairs, spending their own money on materials, from "the harnesses of the huge ore buckets that were part of the tram at the Blistered Horn Mine. The buckets were taken off the harnesses, and a steel frame that held a wooden seat was welded to the harness."

Skiers catch a ride on the first chairlift in Colorado at Pioneer. *Courtesy Crested Butte Mountain Heritage Museum.*

On December 3, 1939, they talked Mrs. Ellen Fordham into being the first passenger on the chair lift, which was named Comet. They told her that if the chair started swaying violently, she should get off. The chair did just that, and she jumped. "Some minor adjustments were made on the slack in the cable and the lift seemed to operate satisfactorily."

The ski area operated from 9:00 a.m. to 5:00 p.m. It cost one dollar a day to ride the lift and fifty cents for members of the ski club. A season ticket cost thirty dollars. Non-skiers could ride the lift for thirty-five cents.

There was a grand opening celebration on March 10, 1940. About 350 people came and bought coffee and hot chocolate for a nickel, hamburgers for ten cents and beer for fifteen cents in the basement of the Pioneer resort lodge. Thor Groswold came and put on an exhibition of skiing. He said that the area was one of the finest in the state and praised the local ski club for its huge accomplishment.

The area operated and held meets for two years. Famous skiers, such as Barney McLean and Barbara Kidder, came to compete.

In 1942, Pioneer shut down for World War II, along with so many other areas in Colorado. An item in the *Steamboat Pilot* reported on the closure:

The Gunnison Ski Club has decided not to operate the Pioneer Ski Course on Cement Creek this winter because of the war conditions, believing that conservation of gasoline and tires will be more essential. One trip will be made to the area on October 24 at which time the chairs will be removed from the ski tow, cables weather proofed and cabins boarded up for the duration. At the same time a forestry truck will be taken to the area to bring back any scrap metal that may be found at the ski course. Gunnison people will enjoy their sport on the college course northeast of Gunnison, snow conditions permitting.[97]

Pioneer reopened in 1946 with a new cabin at the top of the lift for a warming hut. After the war, enrollment went up at WSC, and skiing increased at the area. Collegiate teams began to compete, and the WSC ski team and Gunnison Ski Club held meets there.

Eventually, the WSC ski team wanted a new ski area with a better jump than they had been able to build at Pioneer (it was deemed inadequate and dangerous in 1948). Rozman Hill was created across the highway and a mile north, and the two areas competed for a while.

Pioneer closed down because of financial difficulties, lack of volunteers and problems among ski club members. Also, there was concern about safety and maintenance at Pioneer. An accident in 1948 sealed the fate of the ski area for racing. Joan Trumbull skied out of control on the downhill course and hit poor Ellen Fordham and then the timing shack at about sixty miles per hour. Both of Joan's skis went through the wall of the shack, and it was moved about a foot. She suffered a concussion, a broken leg and a dislocated ankle.

Pioneer operated for one last season in 1952. The rope tow from the beginner's slope went to Rozman Hill, and the chair lift went on to Monarch Pass.

Pershing Ski Hill

This little hill saw a similar growth and decline with the fortunes of the mines as was experienced at Whitepine. The Crested Butte Ski Club in the little mining town north of Gunnison, which is now known as the Wildflower Capital of Colorado, decided to look for a ski hill close to town for the kids. In her thesis, "The Pershing Ski Hill," Lynda K. MacLennan told the story of the little hill located two miles northeast of Crested Butte near the Pershing Mine (GPS 38°52'42"N, 106°59'54"W).[98]

Many of the men who would create the hill worked in the coal mines nearby. They had served under General Pershing during World War II. It's said that they decided to call the hill the Pershing Ski Hill for their general, not the mine. The WSC ski team called it Peanut Hill because it was small and it was both along Peanut Road and near the Peanut Mine. It was 1950, and skiing was even more popular in the state than it had been before the war.

Gifts came in for the creation of the hill, including the parcel of land, which CF&I allowed folks to use during the winter. In the summers, a local named Joe Eccher leased the land for grazing. The ski club had to take down the fences in the fall and put them back up in the spring.

Many people came to help set it up, including the WSC ski team, under the direction of Sven Wiik. They were asked to help build a slalom course and a ski jump. After it was built, there was a big party, and then about one hundred people worked to keep it running. MacLennan shared the story of the tow:

> The tow on the ski hill…came from a practice run at the Pioneer Ski Area. The Model "A" engine was covered with a shack, which was an old coal shed owned by the C.F.&I. The Warming House was a tin shed, which was donated by Joe Saya and moved to the site by the ski club…The Model "A" engine only had enough power to pull two skiers up the hill at once. If three people would try to ride the rope tow at the same time, it would die. Also, different members in the community were in charge of the battery to run the engine. John Somrak and Steve Krizmanich would take turns keeping the battery at their homes. If you wanted to go skiing, you would have to take the battery with you and return it at the end of the day. The reason for removing the battery each time was because of freezing problems, and also because it would disappear from time to time.[99]

The ski jump was most popular and was used for years by WSC, though some skiers said they closed their eyes when they went off the first time. It was reportedly made of wood cribbing and snow, was twenty meters long and was called the "Snow Job." The slalom course was said to be almost too steep, especially for the children. Poles for the course came from nearby trees.

When the CF&I mine closed in 1952, the population of Crested Butte started to decline. Folks went down to Rozman Hill to ski instead.

Beans Krizmanich practices ski jumping on Pershing Hill. *Courtesy Crested Butte Mountain Heritage Museum.*

ROZMAN HILL

This area was about halfway between the Cement Creek Road and Crested Butte on the John Rozman ranch, located west of the highway and across the Snake River (GPS coordinates 38°49'57"N, 106°56'19"W). Student Bob D. Lee told the story of Pioneer in his thesis, "Rozman Hill Ski Area: 'Where's that Angel?'"[100]

After World War II, energy and the drive for skiing came not from the Gunnison Ski Club but from a new group, the collegiate ski team at WSC. Sven Wiik led the team and the effort to find a new hill after Pioneer that would allow development of a real ski program.

Wiik was hired in spite of the fact that he was newly arrived from Sweden and couldn't speak English at all. His strength was Nordic or cross-country skiing, and he really helped to establish it in the United States.

Behind the push for a collegiate program at the school was Crosby Perry-Smith, who had enrolled there after the war. He urged administrators to provide one, convincing them to do so by pointing out that the college would benefit from publicity and that skiing had educational value.

The ski team went looking for a new site where it could develop the collegiate program while also skiing at Pershing Ski Hill. In its search, it asked a few landowners for permission and was turned down by one after another:

Finally, one December evening as the ski team bus passed Rozman Hill, part of Whetstone Mountain near Crested Butte, Adolph Kuss said, "Stop the bus. I think I see a prospect." A quick examination and Kuss said, "I've found us our hill. Now where's the property owner!" What attracted Kuss was a "natural profile for a jumping hill, something that wouldn't cost a lot of money." Wiik talked to John Rozman, owner of the land, and quickly received permission to use the hill. "It was a good mountain, it was accessible from the highway, and the landowner did not object to us being there." Wiik concluded, "...Rozman hill was the place."

The ski team built a jump that first season, which was the 1949–50 season. It chopped down a few trees, filled in an irrigation ditch some and contoured the hill with snow. It was just a 120-foot jump and not up to the highest standards for competition, but it fit the bill for training. The next season, a new jump was built that was better and longer; it was 150 feet. WSC paid for a 550-foot rope tow for that jump from lift fees at Cupola Hill and from the ski instructor program.

The Mountaineers got a 1928 Studebaker coup, put dual wheels on it and strung the rope between them. Adolph Kuss said, "We just backed it up the hill, chained it to a tree, took one wheel off—that was our first tow." The ski team became more ingenious. In 1951, it replaced the Studebaker with lumber trucks, and it built two drive units; the tow was now eight hundred to one thousand feet long and driven from the bottom of the hill.

The lift broke down during the 1951–52 season, and the USFS condemned it and then required certain improvements for the next season, such as a downhill course. The junior chamber of commerce and the Jaycees seemed to have helped the ski team put up a warming hut, which was built with free labor from many members in about a week. They instigated a concession—selling candy, coffee, cake and hot dogs—and held a "bumper safety tape campaign" to pay for it.

The old tow was extended 700 feet, and a new 1100 foot tow was built beyond the old one. The new three-quarter mile downhill run was now serviced by a 2100 foot tow system. However, the racers still had "to walk a quarter of a mile to reach the downhill gate."

A skier balances on Norwegian
snowshoes while a companion watches.
Courtesy of Cardcow.com.

A lad slides downhill on snowshoes.
Courtesy of Cardcow.com.

Left: A poster of
Conquistador hangs
on the wall at the
Hermit Basin Christian
Conference Center
and Resort. *Caryn
Boddie photo.*

Below: Skip Chambers
(right) and John
Buchholz take a break
atop the hill at the Cole
Black Ranch above
the Eagle cemetery,
while Susan Koonce
and friends ski below.
*Courtesy of Eagle County
Historical Society and Eagle
Valley Library.*

Right: Skiers catch a ride on
the chairlift at Conquistador.
*Courtesy of the Hermit Basin Christian
Conference Center and Resort.*

Below: Stanley Rice (squatting) and
Senior Mahoney clown around
at twelve thousand feet on Ajax
Mountain. *Courtesy of Senior Mahoney.*

Above: The Creede ski hill was still visible in 2014. *Peter Boddie photo.*

Left: A chair from the chair lift at Cuchara has been aged by weather, not by use. *Caryn Boddie photo.*

Right: An ad in a winter issue of *Colorado Wonderland* magazine extols the ski virtues of the state. *Caryn Boddie collection.*

Below: The residents of Creede enjoyed their town hill. *Photo courtesy of Mines and Memories, Creede.*

Above: A sign for Ski Dallas at Sams, Colorado, was preserved. *Caryn Boddie photo.*

Left: A low-tech T-bar at Ski Dallas did the job. *Peter Boddie photo.*

Top: Skiers line up at Glenwood Mountain Park on Red Mountain in the 1950s. *Photo courtesy of the Frontier Historical Museum.*

Bottom: Peter Boddie perches in the Dodge truck that powered the rope tow at Top O' La Veta, with the runs in the background. *Caryn Boddie photo.*

Hollyhocks were still growing in 2014 near the Whittaker Ranch ski hill. *Peter Boddie photo.*

Sugarite was loved by the locals on both sides of the Colorado–New Mexico border. *Courtesy Arthur Johnson Memorial Library, Raton.*

Robert, Richard and Gerry at Hesperus, circa 1963. *Courtesy of Robert McDaniel.*

Red Mountain still bears orange lift towers from lost ski areas. *Caryn Boddie photo.*

Above: The Redstone Ski Area still looks inviting from the road. *Caryn Boddie photo.*

Left: Faded instructions grace the lift shack at Redstone Ski Area. *Caryn Boddie photo.*

An ad in the 1953 winter issue of *Colorado Wonderland* enticed skiers to the state. *Caryn Boddie collection.*

Poster shows that the U.S. Forest Service has always played a role in helping folks to ski on national forest land. *Peter Boddie photo.*

Ski equipment is always evolving. *Caryn Boddie photo.*

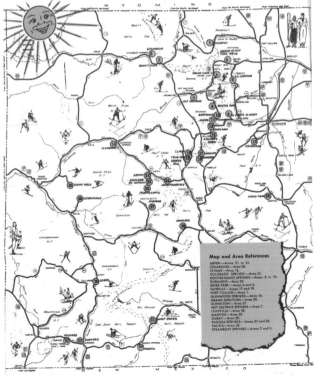

This map from a 1951 winter issue of *Colorado Wonderland* shows where the ski areas were that year. *Caryn Boddie collection.*

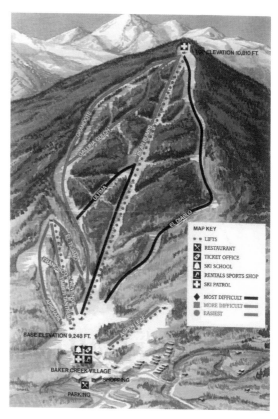

A ski map shows the runs at Cuchara. *Courtesy of Coloradoskihistory.com.*

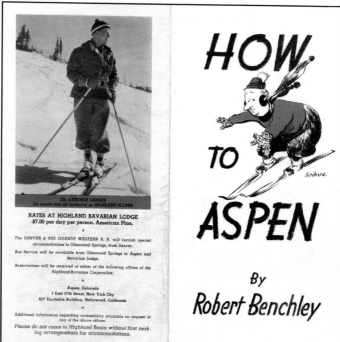

Robert Benchley, an American humorist, created a brochure for the Highland Bavarian venture. *Aspen Historical Society.*

This Mutoscope card of a lovely skier was created by Billy DeVorss in the 1940s. It was entitled "Red White and You" and was part of the American Girls series. *Caryn Boddie collection.*

This postcard of Aspen Mountain shows Ruthie's Run, the wide run on the right. Roch Run is the narrow run just to the left of it in the trees and runs into Corkscrew at the bottom. *Caryn Boddie collection.*

Above: A postcard shows skiing at different areas of Colorado. *Caryn Boddie collection.*

Right: An ad from the Christmas 1954 *Colorado Wonderland* shows a variety of ways to ski the state. *Caryn Boddie collection.*

SKI COLORADO

52 tows or lifts serving unlimited slopes in 33 developed areas

10,000 square miles of powder snow

november into june

ski in the sun

Send for NEW Free SKI FOLDER →

Colorado Winter Sports Committee
Room 204—Capitol Building
Denver 2, Colorado

YES... I want your NEW Free, full color Ski Folder and Map, "Ski Colorado" with detailed area descriptions plus calendar of Ski Events.

NAME

ADDRESS

CITY   STATE

COLORADO
colorado climate...
the magic ingredient

SKI
COLORADO
THIS YEAR
**Make this your year to discover how much fun
a ski vacation can be!**

Over 10,000 square miles of light-as-fluff powder snow, sparkling in the bright sunshine of Colorado's crisp, dry climate, offers you skiing you never dreamed possible. And you can enjoy Colorado's perfect snow conditions no matter what your skiing ability, for every ski area in Colorado offers a wide variety of runs—from gentle novice, perfect for learning or practicing, to spectacular expert, dropping from the very peaks of the lofty Rockies. And over 60 high-speed lifts and tows in Colorado keep lift lines short—you get all the skiing you want!

Choose from a wide selection of accommodations in every price range . . . including attractive all-expense package plans offered by many lodges.

Don't put it off another season—come to Colorado this year and discover how much fun a ski vacation can be!

COLORADO WINTER SPORTS COMMITTEE
Room 329, Capitol Building, Denver 2, Colorado

This one coupon brings full information about Colorado's skiing.

Name _____

Address _____

City _____ Zone ___ State ___

**MAIL COUPON TODAY
FOR COMPLETE INFORMATION**

Free full-color ski folder; detailed information on all Colorado ski areas, lodges and transportation schedules (including prices); and complete list of winter sports events.

Left: An ad from an issue of *Colorado Wonderland* in the late 1950s invites skiers to the state. *Caryn Boddie collection.*

Below: Folks take a breather at the base of the Mancos Hill ski course. *Courtesy of Janelle Beaber.*

A Nordic skier concentrates during a race at Rozman Hill. *Courtesy Crested Butte Mountain Heritage Museum.*

The relationship with rancher John Rozman was very positive; he was generous because he wanted to help the ski team and the community (the team agreed to pay him one dollar to make it legal). Coach Sven Wiik was right there to fix any problems the presence of skiing caused on the ranch;

While looking for his landing, a jumper sails at Rozman Hill. *Courtesy Crested Butte Mountain Heritage Museum.*

and Rozman could see that Wiik was devoted to the development of the team. This made it possible for WSC to really develop its skiers there.

Rozman Hill served WSC and the community from the 1949–50 season to the 1962–63 season. The cross-country trails were liked by everyone, but the jumping hill was not. It was deemed inadequate by more than one good jumper. The downhill course was thought to be too narrow and short. By 1953, folks were complaining about the facility, and by 1955, it was apparent that the public needed another hill. Plus, the rope tows at Rozman Hill were infamous; one was called "Man Killer."

> *To ride "Man Killer" was an exhausting task! At times many skiers did not have the strength to hold on for 1,000 feet. Then, too, the tows literally attempted to be "killers." They snatched and tangled scarves, jackets, and loose articles of clothing in the ropes. Another problem with the tows was that the safety gates did not always work properly…Dick Flaherty remembered one such dangerous situation when a young boy became caught in one of the tows. The rope was twisted around his jacket, and he was being dragged toward the turn wheel. Flaherty and his friend, Jerry McMillan, while skiing the downhill course saw the problem, raced over, pulled themselves hand over hand up the rope tow. McMillan was able to trip the safety gate as the boy was about to enter the turn wheel.*

A ski rider enjoys the Rozman Hill jump. *Courtesy Crested Butte Mountain Heritage Museum.*

Skiers before or after a day of skiing at Rozman Hill. *WSCU archives, Leslie J. Savage Library, Western State Colorado University.*

Some thought that the rope tow should be replaced with a J-bar or T-bar, but that never happened because no one had the money, and there was talk of Crested Butte being developed.

The ski team moved up there, and Rozman shut down.

MARBLE SKI AREA

Northern Gunnison County reaches over McClure Pass and into a gorgeous valley where the Crystal River flows. There, south from Carbondale past Chair Mountain, is the town of Marble. From the town up the Carbonate Creek drainage is the site of the Marble Ski Area (GPS coordinates 39°5'10"N, 107°11'0"W). It was one of those sad and confusing places, where developers planned not a ski hill or a ski area but a large resort—and it went bust before it really got going.

Collegiate ski team members benefitted from the development of ski racing at the college level in Gunnison County. This 1970s racer was a member of the University of Denver ski team. *Courtesy of University of Denver Special Collections and Archives.*

Some say it really was a grand idea; others say it was a scam from inception. It's not clear which is closest to the real story—some even say a curse on the valley by Native Americans doomed the project from the beginning.

Vince Savage, editor of *Marble Chips*, the newsletter of the Marble Historical Society, wrote the story:

> *The history of the Marble Ski Area is one rife with rumor, ambiguity, conflict, fraud and bankruptcy. Is it the Ute curse, or does such scenery create craziness? Maybe since the view is so "unbelievable" yet real,*

The chairlift at Marble Ski Area never saw much use. *Courtesy Marble Museum.*

it encourages "those with more dollars than sense" to seek believers in
appearances rather than in truth. Whatever the influences, the first
documented intention to create a downhill ski area at Marble began
with a December 5, 1963 headline in the Glenwood Sage stating
"Rumors Rife on Ski Area at Marble." By Christmas 1963, "rumors
that a ski area might be going in above Marble were officially confirmed
as Mr. and Mrs. Howard Stroud announced that negotiations for the

sale of their 1500 acre Marble Ranch to a Denver developer are currently underway."[101]

Jim Nelson also wrote about the star-crossed fortunes of the ski area in *Marble & Redstone: A Quick History*:

> *The Oberlander Corporation of Denver purchased 1,500 acres around Marble in 1964, announcing intentions of developing a ski area and summer resort northeast of town…Marble was, it was reasoned, "blessed" with an abundance of snow every winter…Marble seemed to possess the requisite ingredients for a snow-oriented resort.*[102]

The following five years brought various proposals, but eventually the area did open. According to coloradoskihistory.com, "Marble Ski Resort opened for the [1970–71] ski season with only snowcats. The following year they contracted Riblet to install a double chair up the main run."[103]

Marble Chips reads, "For the 1971–72 season skiing was offered on weekends only by reservation with adult lift tickets $3 and $2 for children 12 and under."

However, two locals the authors spoke with who had skied the area don't remember ever paying, as they always got a free ticket or knew someone who worked there. No one seemed certain whether the area really ever opened to paying customers and the general public. They said that although the area got lots of snow, the southwest exposure made for inconsistent conditions and not very good skiing.

The reasons for the failure of the area were many: the ski hill was on a west/southwest-facing slope, developers lacked the necessary funding for a large area and townspeople stood in opposition to ski area plans.

The environmental movement was gaining momentum in the 1970s, and people didn't want runs cut through virgin timber. The town incorporated, and residents created the Crystal Valley Environmental Protection Association to fight the project.

The U.S. Forest Service never seemed to be too keen on the idea either, as the planned area would extend onto the national forest. Kim Boddie, who worked in the U.S. Forest Service office in Carbondale at the time, recalled how the original lift, supposedly built on private land, extended a short distance onto the national forest, and the USFS made the ski people shorten it.

To top it all off, the earth started moving up Carbonate Creek; two mudslides within a week in 1973 roared downhill, sounding like a freight train, carrying tons of silt, rocks, trees and other debris into town and clogging culverts. A May 14 slide affected the ski complex when "part of an area the land developers originally had planned for multifamily dwelling units, gave way, tearing out 100 feet of the private road leading to the ski area facilities and covering part of a county road before pouring into Beaver Lake."[104]

As things fell apart, financial dealings were questioned. The area was sold and sold again. In 2014, it was in the hands of Ken Goode, who was working on the area.

"Who knows," wrote Savage, "maybe in time, those three-dollar lift tickets will be available to locals or at least the privileged 'old timers.'"

The ski area is located on private land behind a locked gate, but as of 2014, a local outfitter had access to the property and included it on some of its tours, at least in the summer. Just ask in town.

11

Saguache County

Unique Ride Up a Special Hill

*When the train was ready to leave for Gunnison it was found that two women
and a girl were missing. They were later brought down on a helper engine.*
—Steamboat Pilot, *1938*[105]

In 1881, the Denver and Rio Grande Railroad laid narrow-gauge track
up and over Marshall Pass in an effort to beat the Denver and South Park
Railroad into Gunnison country. Dr. Duane Vandenbusche told the story
with pictures and captions in *Around Monarch Pass*. He wrote, "Key in the
Rio Grande's victory were snowsheds on both sides of Marshall Pass, which
protected trains from high winds and drifting snow."[106] The train ran for
seventy-four years, until 1955.

In the middle of that span, the train became a ski lift.

MARSHALL PASS

Skiing at Marshall Pass took place mostly on the west side, where there
was steeper terrain and better snow. Skiers could be dropped off by train
at the top of the pass (GPS coordinates 38°23'30"N, 106°14'55"W) and
ski different routes, up to a mile in length, all of which funneled to a
stream crossing and switchback on the train route below. There was also
a warming hut.

Skiers take a break at the summit of Marshall Pass. *Courtesy of Dr. Duane Vandenbusche.*

Abbott Fay said that Thor Groswold and T.J. Flynn of Aspen went on the first trip:

> *Embers of the old Gunnison Ski Club were fanned to life again in 1938,*
> *when three Gunnison men, Wes McDermott, Rial Lake, and Charles*
> *Schweitzer, planned a special excursion train to Marshall Pass, between*
> *Gunnison and Salida…The train itself served as a ski lift as the crowd*
> *zoomed down to the water tank at Shawano, 700 feet below the summit,*
> *and then were hauled back to the top for another run.*[107]

The *Aspen Daily Times* reported on the first official trip:

> *More than 500 persons participated in the formal opening of the ski courses*
> *on the slopes of Angel and Shavano mountains on Marshall Pass Sunday.*
> *Special excursion trains, which taxed the passenger carrying equipment*
> *of the Rio Grande narrow-[gauge] lines, carried snow sports enthusiasts*
> *from Salida and Gunnison. More than 400 persons from Salida and 100*
> *from Gunnison made the trip. Ticket applications from about 200 snow*
> *fans were turned down due to lack of railroad equipment accommodations.*
> *Count Phillipe de Pret, Belgian nobleman, accompanied the Gunnison*
> *delegation. The count gave instructions at the Western State College on*
> *Friday and Saturday of last week.*[108]

According to the *Steamboat Pilot*, "At the formal opening of the Marshall Pass ski course last Sunday two girls were injured on a toboggan slide, one suffered several dislocated vertebrae and the other a broken leg."[109] Also, they lost the few who were brought down later.

Another newspaper wrote about the excursion:

> The *Gunnison Courier* states that over 600 persons went on the special ski train to the top of Marshall [P]ass last Sunday. Some had home-made skis and other[s] the finest outfits obtainable to help in the formal opening of the Marshall [P]ass ski course. The Gunnison special carried skis, poles, clothes, goggles. It stopped in the snowshed. A course had been cleared of trees and stumps for a distance of two and a half miles...The program was arranged by the Salida and Gunnison Winter Sports clubs.[110]

It's not clear how many trips were made to Marshall Pass with skiers. However, the narrow gauge went out of favor, and the standard became the chosen gauge. Western State College football players helped railroad personnel pull up the tracks in 1955, and the railroad bed became a gravel road that was not maintained in winter.

12

Custer County

Glass Half Full for the Folks

We did have a snow packer. It was 8 feet long with bicycle rims on each end. Redwood slats were fastened from rim to rim. A big T framework attached to the front to pull it. I think my dad may have come up with this invention from some medieval torture machine.
—George Brodin, 2014[111]

The country between the Wet Mountains and the Sangre de Cristo Range, known as the Wet Mountain Valley, is home to the charming towns of Westcliffe and Silver Cliff. It's a beautiful area that still hosts cross-country skiers in the winter but is visited most in summers by concert goers, fishermen and hikers.

Hal Walter penned a column about the ski history of the area. He wrote, "People have tried again and again to make skiing work here and it just hasn't. The lack of snow in some years—accompanied by the bounty of extreme winds—makes skiing marginal here."[112]

However, the few areas in the county actually had some positives, at least for the regular people who enjoyed skiing them.

ALVARADO

It is said that the first ski area in Custer County was located near Alvarado Campground (GPS coordinates 38°4'37"N, 105°34'0"W) and that the owner of the area was killed in an accident with his machinery. Not much else is known. The authors were able to locate the area from a 1953 aerial photograph, which clearly indicates a telltale straight line through the trees for a lift and two ski runs. By 2014, however, the runs had almost completely grown in with aspens and were difficult to hike up from the nearby campground. There was very little evidence left to indicate that people had once skied there.

Ski San Isabel

This area operated for almost three decades, from 1956 to 1985. It was located in the Wet Mountains near Bigelow (GPS coordinates 38°5'40"N, 105°7'11"W). Peter Bronski wrote, "There was a 1300-foot-long rope tow—actually two rope tows attached to the same set of poles. Electric motors provided enough juice to carry 13 people up the slope at a time. There were two runs: right and left, and very little elevation gain."[113]

During its time, the people who came to use it were mostly families from Pueblo, and they came to learn the basics of skiing. There were steel workers, doctors, farmers, teachers, plumbers and others. They enjoyed music that was broadcast from a speaker mounted on a tree, polka music being the most popular. According to Bronski, "It was a family gathering place where kids could be turned loose to play and watched by all, and everyone could hang out and enjoy the camaraderie."[114]

George Brodin remembered working at the area. His detailed account, published in *Pueblo Lore*, gave an especially good picture of what the small areas of the day were like and what those working there did to make them run:

> *As I understand it, at that time, if you took payment for anything under one dollar, you did not have to deal with sales tax. The lift ticket price was set at 99 cents and my brother, sister and I were the primary ticket sellers. The parking was on the sides of the highway well above the base of the ski area. We met the skiers as they came through the barbed-wire cattle gate to gain access to the ski hill. Armed with a hand stamp and a roll of pennies, we gallantly sold lift tickets knowing full well the consequences of not giving the penny back and "cheating" the customer. We never raised the price, but later went to paper tickets that were visible and attached to a zipper or coat ring by a string.*

In the mornings, my dad, Kenny Bozell or me, when I was old enough, would walk up the hill, carefully laying the rope on the ground from the pegs we hung it on to prevent it from freezing to the ground overnight. Once we reached the top we would place the safety gate in place. Originally this was a 2 x 4 holding a rocker switch down; later, we used an extension cord that would be unhooked if a skier didn't let go or got tangled in the rope and dragged near the motors. The main switch would be thrown to stop the motor.

The first person up would bring skis so you didn't have to walk back down. The next action was generally to turn the heat lamp on to warm up the record player. Occasionally the needle would stick, and the rope tow was so slow that a "hot time," "a hot time," "a hot time," "a hot time," "a hot time," would seem to go on forever as we all scrambled to get to the turn table and encourage the needle along.

Closing was always better than opening, it was less work to come back down the hill after turning off the motors and skiing from pole to pole, hanging the rope off the ground for the night.

The walk up to the car was a bit of a task though. The road was a good 100 feet up from the base of the ski tow. This seemed like climbing Mt. Everest for a 10- or 12-year-old after skiing all day. Many people would simply drive up to watch the skiers. One time my dad counted nearly 100 cars. We had truly hit the big time...

Ski instruction was performed in a fairly casual manner. My dad would say, "Ken or George or Neil (any number of high school kids were pressed into service) why don't you take this person up the hill and show her how to turn and stop..." The original warming hut was located in a sheltered spot on the windward side of a stand of Aspen trees. It was approximately 10-feet wide, 18-feet long and sloped from 10-feet to 8-feet high...

Heat was provided by a 55-gallon drum-barrel wood stove. The hut was disassembled and moved to the bottom after a couple of years to accommodate the non-skiers who came to watch but were not inclined to walk halfway up the hill to the warming hut.

There was a two-seat "biffy" with his and her sides. There was never any vending or food for sale while under the operation of the Brodin Family, though pots of homemade chili, soup and various "Bo John" and Italian food were nearly always found warming or simmering on the barrel stove. We all shared at lunch time.[115]

The ski area shut down in 1985 shortly after the owners of the area were turned down for a loan from the Small Business Administration.

Conquistador

The largest ski area in Custer County was Conquistador, located about five miles west of Westcliffe in the Sangre de Cristo Range (GPS coordinates 38°7'3"N, 105°35'6"W). In 2014, it was clearly visible from town. Like many ambitious ski resort projects, financial troubles knocked this area down, and other troubles kept it on the mat.

A flier advertises Conquistador. *Courtesy Dorothy Urban, Silver Cliff Museum.*

According to Brad Chamberlin, who created coloradoskihistory.com, the area operated from 1976 to 1988 and from 1992 to 1993. Dick Milstein, who had worked on other ski areas, had a dream of a resort situated in southern Colorado. He was the driving force behind Conquistador. Chamberlin wrote:

> *Conquistador opened in 1976 with two small pony lifts and limited terrain. The ski area was not very popular with local residents of Custer County. Mr. Milstein said, "I had some great people in the valley backing [the area] and a lot of people fighting it. There were a lot of ranchers there that didn't want it."*
>
> *"...A major expansion was executed. The resort purchased and installed a double and triple chair from Doppelmayr USA, located in Golden, Colorado. This expansion along with a new snowmaking system, and a decently sized lodge, put Conquistador on the map for skiing in the state. Resort officials also had approval to expand south and west of the existing terrain.*[116]

Financial troubles soon followed. Christopher Kolomitz wrote, "Almost as soon as the expansions were complete, the bank, which gained $23 million in loans from the Small Business Administration for use at Conquistador and other projects, was in default. In late 1982, the SBA took over ownership of the mountain."[117]

In 1986, *Sangre Magazine* painted a picture of the area:

> *As the Conquistadores knew, there is more to conquering a mountain than going up. Once you hit the top of the lift it can be a real rodeo. Twelve trails offer a variety of skiable terrain. Named for famous cattle brands and western routes, 30% of the runs are beginner, 55% intermediate and 15% expert. That adds up to good skiing for every level of skier in the family.*[118]

Milstein left the project, and the government ran the resort at a loss until 1988. Some eighty jobs were lost to the community when the area closed that year.

An investor from California named Mund Shaikly and Ray McEnhill from England purchased the resort for $3 million and ran it for one year under the name Mountain Cliffe, but snow was scarce. They were going to keep developing it; however, conflicts between the owners and management team they'd hired proved to be the last straw, and it was closed. The property was sold again in 1995.

SILVER HILLS

This area was located east of Westcliffe along Colorado Highway 96, a few miles past Querida (GPS coordinates 38°9'46"N, 105°14'17"W).

Coloradoskihistory.com reports that the owners of the nearby Singing Acres Ranch ran the area for nearly twenty years (1966–84). Their names were Clara Reida and Margaret Locarnini. It had a rental shop, a lodge, a rope tow and a J-bar. "The J-bar was made in Austria before World War II and was originally installed at Camp Hale, then later at Cuchara, and finally at Silver Hills."[119] Children learned to ski on the hill with the local 4H Club, and it was a great place for kids, according to John N., who commented on the website.

13

Huerfano County

Skiing for Families—On Again, Off Again

Folks in this rural mountain valley have watched their local ski area open and close so many times that they sometimes feel as if they are living through a real-life version of the movie Groundhog Day.
—Colorado Springs Gazette, *2008*[120]

Two ski areas provided family fun for a few decades after World War II: one was on top of a pass in the Sangre de Cristo Range and the other was in the Cucharas River Valley, near the highway.

Years later, another ski area was opened in the valley of the Cucharas, south of the first one. That one opened and closed and opened and closed, leaving people shaking their heads.

CUCHARA SKI BASIN

This area was open for about two decades, from the 1950s to the 1970s, and it had five runs and a vertical of 350 feet, according to coloradoskihistory. com. It was located just a half mile north of Cuchara (GPS coordinates 37°23'14"N, 105°5'59"W). It operated first with a rope tow and later with a platter lift that was 2,100 feet long and pulled four hundred skiers per hour.[121]

Norma Lou Murr of Walsenburg said, "It was fine with a rope tow. It was fine when you were going up like that, and that's how we started…You'd go up on a rope tow, turn around and come down. And, of course, then you want bigger and better."[122] She and her husband, Floyd Murr, were involved in Cuchara Ski Basin and Top O' La Veta. "He loved to ski, so he was the one getting all the little ski courses going."

In 2014, after Floyd had passed away, Norma Lou talked with the authors. She said that they'd drive to La Veta then go up to Cuchara. Right as they went in the valley, they'd go across a meadow and up. The tow was on the land of a farmer named Goemmer.

Cuchara Basin was written up as "especially suited for family winter fun" in at least two issues of the *Manual of Colorado Skiing and Winter Sports* (ski seasons 1961–62 and 1963–64). The reports read, "Large open basin affording acres of beginners' slopes…An ideal family ski area with ski school offering special student group rates."[123]

Tickets were $2.50 per day for adults and $1.25 for children under fourteen. There were special rates for groups. The season was from November to mid-April, and the area operated on weekends and holidays. There was a shelter house at the top of the runs, along with rentals and a restaurant. Folks could stay in a motel or cabins for $3.00 to $15.00.

Murr said that a German professor who was teaching at Adams State College learned about what was going on at Cuchara Basin, came down and got very excited. She remembered his name as Dr. Bucher. He taught the Murr children to ski, and they were so excited when they learned to turn around with a kick turn.

A lack of snow and financial troubles may have caused the closure of the area in 1970 or 1971, reports coloradoskihistory.com.

Top O' La Veta

In 1960, when the eldest son was ten, the Murr family started skiing at this area, which was near the ghost town at the summit of the Old La Veta Pass (GPS coordinates 37°35'11"N, 105°12'11"W) called Up Top. The ski area opened about that time.

A website for the town of La Veta tells the basics:

After World War II, returning servicemen wanted a place for their families to ski. The land's original homeowner from 1917, Juan Antonio Trujillo gave permission to start a small ski resort complete with a warming hut, privey

One wheel from the rope tow set up at Top of La Veta rests in the lush grass. *Caryn Boddie photo.*

[sic] and ticket booth. A Chevy truck was donated to run a rope tow up the hill. Local children and adults had great fun learning the basics of skiing. Today the Chevy truck is all that remains of the once booming ski area.[124]

Murr said the area probably operated for two years. When Taos Ski Valley Resort opened, the Murrs decided that they'd had quite enough of helping to operate ski hills, and they started skiing there, along with other folks.

PANADERO OR CUCHARA VALLEY SKI AREA

Located to the southwest of Cuchara off of Colorado Highway 12 (GPS coordinates 37°20'57"N, 105°7'28"W), the Cuchara Valley Ski Area, also known as Panadero, is absolutely beautiful, which lends more sadness to its troubled history.

Trying again and again to get it right is only part of the story of this area, which first opened in 1981 and closed for the last of several times in 2000. Another aspect is that most of the owners were not really passionate about skiing; they were real estate investors. It's been really kind of heartbreaking because the people who live in Huerfano County could use a successful ski area for the economic benefits it would bring.

In 2008, residents banded together in a nonprofit cooperative effort to open the ski area again. Steve Perkins, retired chief executive officer of Huerfano County Medical Center and president of the cooperative, told the story to the *Colorado Springs Gazette.* "We've seen a lot of people come in and try to make quick money on real estate, or by flipping the property…We haven't seen people trying to manage this sustainably for the long-term good of the region. That's what we want to do."[125] The cooperative was hoping to open skiing on the forty private acres at the base of the area, not on U.S. Forest Service land, initially. This and other cooperative efforts failed, and the ski area remained closed for the 2014–15 ski season.

Dwight Harrison ran the ski area for four years, including its opening in 1981, when it was called Panadero. The Monument resident said in 2008 that the area could work if it was run as a small area.[126]

Locals weren't involved in the initial development; reportedly, Texas developers owned it. They planned to sell land and lots for housing, a total of 130 lots on twenty-three tracts in three filings. A series of

Lifts and runs at beautiful Cuchara are lost to skiers. *Caryn Boddie photo.*

A sign welcomes visitors to a lost resort. *Peter Boddie photo.*

Texans bought the area, ran it for short periods of time—sometimes with success—then closed it and sold it. The season of 1999–2000 was the area's last, but the area was not dismantled. Residents eventually offered to pledge their own money to make the area operate with a low-cost lease. However, the U.S. Forest Service had become reluctant to issue a new permit.

The district ranger for the forest at Cuchara has said that he would have to do some serious thinking before giving another permit for Cuchara. "We have never said no, but we need to be convinced there is long-term management with a good plan."[127]

In 2012, the owner, Bruce Cantrell, was selling Cuchara for $4.5 million. He said the only way the area would succeed was for it to become a year-round resort with attractions besides skiing, such as a zip line.

14

Las Animas County

Family Hill at the State Line

We used to just shoot water in the air and, if all the conditions were right, hope it would come down as snow.
—Millard Walton, 1982[128]

There once was a coal-mining town called Sugarite in the Raton Basin, which "extends from Cimarron, New Mexico, northeastward to Huerfano Park, Colorado, about 100 mi long and as much as 60 mi wide."[129] The name of the town, which became the name of a ski area, is said to be an Anglicized version of the word *chicarica*, Spanish for "chicory."

Around 1900, Robert and Ruth Walton came to the area from Tennessee in a covered wagon and settled on what became known as Walton's Mountain. "Robert enjoyed the green, peaceful meadows nestled amid the towering mesas. Succeeding generations have found the locale to their liking as well."[130] At some time after their arrival, they must have started skiing, because skiing and ski areas became a big part of the family story.

SUGARITE OR RATON BASIN SKI AREA

This ski area is less than a mile north of the state line in Colorado (GPS coordinates 37°0'12"N, 104°20'38"W) but mostly served the community of Raton and, by rights, might be considered a New Mexico ski area.

Raton Ski Basin served people in both Colorado and New Mexico, but it was located just over the border in Colorado. *Courtesy Arthur Johnson Memorial Library, Raton.*

The Walton family, a ranching family, created a ski area on the mountain and worked hard to keep it operating, with the entire family working at the area. In 1982, Pierre Autry told the story for the *Raton Range*:

Much later, in 1960, LaBelle and Millard Walton, along with family and friends, built a one-room warming hut which served as both kitchen

*and rental shop. Familiar sights in the early years on the slopes were cable
bindings and the worn out fingers of gloves caused from gripping the heaving
hemp of a rope tow.*

*Progress occurs, though, even in the outbacks at Walton's Mountain.
The warming hut has given way to a large two-story lodge. The rope tow
has been retired and replaced by a [P]oma and a double-chair lift, which
have proved less wearing on both the glove and the body. In the rental shop,
cable bindings and wood skis have been superceded by a new generation of
safer, step-in style bindings and superior metal-fiberglass composite skis.*

*Snowmaking facilities have been installed to supplement mother nature's
own bounty of what skiers want most—snow.*[131]

The snowmaking technology that the Waltons used in the 1980s was far
more sophisticated than what they used on their first tries to make snow.
They used Snowmaster turbines, which made powder in a wide range of
weather conditions. The area also had a snack bar, a lounge, entertainment
and night skiing.

Bret Heider of Raton, New Mexico, talked with the authors. He had
worked in a coal mine for twenty-five years and then for the Sheriff's Office
and was driving a truck for UPS in 2014. He painted a good picture of skiing
at the area and of the importance of it to locals:

*I skied up at the Raton ski lodge probably from 1970 until it closed…We
used to take ski trips up there through our school and it was a great place
to learn to ski. It was not a big resort but it was easy; everybody who skied
at Angel Fire and Taos, around there, probably learned to ski at Raton ski
lodge…You could rent skis and everything up there. Originally, they only
had a Poma lift. Then, I don't remember the year, but they eventually kept
getting bigger and bigger, more people, and they put a chairlift up towards the
rimrock…It was just a great place to go skiing and we even had night skiing
up there. They had the lights for us and all…The ski trips you'd take a bus
but then you got in high school and everybody drove their own vehicle up there.
It was only a 15-minute drive from Raton, depending on the weather. Back
then it used to snow a lot, not like now…They used to have dances; great
place to go for dances as you got older…In fact, one of my dates in high school
was for the Homecoming that's where we went to eat our dinner was up at the
ski lodge. Chicarica we called it, Chicarica Steak House.*

*It was always fun because everybody from Raton knows everybody…It
was great back in the day.*[132]

Heider also remembered that the first time people got on the Poma lift, they'd sit down and fall down onto the snow; they had to learn to stand up and let it pull them up the hill.

Financial pressures caused the Waltons to sell the 2,200-acre, seventeen-run ski area with 825 feet of vertical in 1989 to a Florida company, which did not open the ski area and didn't even make payments to the bank, causing two foreclosures. The Waltons tried to redeem the property and find a manager to run the area.

A friend of the Waltons tried to get the area going again. Todd Wildermuth said of the hopeful reopening:

> The defunct Sugarite Ski Basin sits on the verge of a new era...The desirable Colorado mountain valley property about 15 miles northeast of Raton quietly slipped away a little more than a month ago from Millard and LaBelle Watson, whose family had owned the land for more than a century.
>
> Now the ski basin, which hasn't operated for the last three winters, is in the hands of Juan P. Garcia, who was born, raised and worked in Raton...A friend of the Walton family for 12 years, Garcia would like to see the ski area reopened to regain the popularity it once enjoyed with Raton skiers and other winter recreation seekers. [133]

In the end, the Walton family not only lost the area but also, sadly, lost their ranch. However, Lynette Walton wrote a letter to the editor of the *Raton Range* expressing her pride in her "hard-working rancher father" who dared greatly. His efforts gave a lot of enjoyment to folks near Raton, on both sides of the state line.

15

Rio Grande County

Racing Down a Town Hill

A freighter named Brockman recently brought his horses from Summitville to Baker's station on snow shoes. The shoes were made of wood, two inches thick, eight inches wide and eighteen inches long, and were fastened to the horses feet by means of wires and straps. The shoes were fastened on, and after a few days of practice in Summitville, the horses learned the modus operandi of the scheme, and on Monday Mr. Brockman rode one horse out over from fifty to one hundred feet of snow, while the second horse pulled a sled loaded with provisions over the same course.
—Rocky Mountain Sun, *1884*[134]

This county is called the gateway to the San Juan Mountains. It features scenic landscapes with many thirteen-thousand-foot peaks. South of the towns in the valley and into the mountains was Summitville, a mining town where many Swedes lived and that had its own newspaper, according to Louise Coldville at the Rio Grande County Museum.[135]

Towns dot the portion of the county that is the San Luis Valley, including Monte Vista, Del Norte and South Fork, which were developed along the railroad and the Rio Grande. Del Norte is the county seat and home to a little-known ski hill.

The Del Norte town ski hill was a little steep. *Peter Boddie photo.*

DEL NORTE HILL

On the southern edge of the town, there is a hill with a big *D* on it (GPS coordinates 37°40'29"N, 106°21'27"W). This is where locals created a ski hill to train ski racers and save the drive up to Wolf Creek.

Johnny R. Chavez, who lives at the foot of the hill, remembered skiers on it. He said that there was a shack on the hill and a rope tow that went nearly to the top.[136] The skiers would zip down the hill and jump back on the rope tow.

According to Coldville, Richard Boyce was in the ski patrol and involved with racing at Wolf Creek Pass. He was in charge of the Del Norte Hill and enabled racers to practice closer to home in the valley, when there was enough snow.

16

Mineral County

Mining, Ski Clubs and Snow

Snow, snow, beautiful snow, has been with us for the past two weeks, falling for a short time; then the sun comes out, and you can possibly imagine the rest, but I doubt it.
—James Cantlin, "Creede," 1892[137]

It was a tough living in winter for the people who lived in the mining towns—Creede, Jimtown, South Creede, Creedmore and Wason—with all

of the snow and isolation. You would presume that it was a little easier in the farming communities in the San Luis Valley; however, people from both places needed to have themselves a little fun. When skiing appeared in the 1930s, they jumped at the chance for winter amusement. They started out at Wolf Creek, and thirty years later, they also skied in Creede.

WOLF CREEK PASS

Skiing at this area really started when the new highway was completed. The old hill was located at the top of the pass (GPS coordinates 37°29'1"N, 106°47'53"W), just about on the Continental Divide (not lower on the east side, where it is now).

It was a big deal to finish the road and to keep it open in winter. In fact, as reported in the *Steamboat Pilot*, a couple of local fathers almost died trying in 1931.[138] The state did manage to get the pass open and keep it open in following years.

Opposite: Miners drive teams of horses pulling mine sleds, circa 1940. *Courtesy of Creede Historical Society.*

Below: The early Wolf Creek Pass area was right on top on the north side. *Courtesy Charles A. Harbert.*

Charles Elliott skied the area in 1934 with a friend as soon as the road first opened to the top. They took homemade wooden skis up and skied straight down. That experience started Elliott's love of skiing, which would last all his life. In 2014, Elliott was 101 years old; he had skied in 2013 on his 100th birthday.

The *Monte Vista Journal* told the story in 2011 when Elliott was ninety-eight and inducted into the Colorado Ski and Snowboard Hall of Fame:

> *From 1936 to 1944, Elliott was the driving force behind an incredible growth and interest in skiing in the San Luis Valley region. His accomplishments during this time include construction of shelter facilities, fundraisers, establishment and training of a local Ski Patrol to increase safety on the mountain, installation of rope tows, exploration of the Wolf Creek Ski Area and hosting of international skiers, not to mention serving as the coordinator for the early operations of the Wolf Creek Ski Area.* [139]

In 1936, the new way of skiing, Alpine skiing, came to Mineral County, and Elliott learned to use poles and to turn. At that time, Elliott said, people in the San Luis Valley communities of Del Norte, Monte Vista and Alamosa were getting interested. "Each one had a little ski club, you know, and the courier newspaper suggested they all make one big area, get a real good ski area started. And I think the little clubs kind of got together." [140] In 1937, they created the San Luis Valley Ski Association and focused on Wolf Creek Pass.

Norm Vance said that those clubs made the first area happen:

> *The inspired bunch of volunteers (and they were all volunteers) who built the first ski runs at Wolf Creek were a hearty bunch who loved skiing and the mountains. I once heard a skier say that skiing was like flying off a mountain with the world wrapped around him. Maybe this is a good description.* [141]

In 1938, the Colorado Department of Highways kept the pass open all winter, and many skiers came to the hill. An item in the *Aspen Daily Times* read, "The Wolf Creek Pass area on the Rio Grande National Forest was used by 3,200 people and had its first big season due to the fact that the road was kept open." [142]

Kelly Boyce installed a rope tow on the north side of the pass near the summit that was powered by an old Chevy truck, and folks paid one dollar per ticket, according to coloradoskihistory.com. The next summer, the

Civilian Conservation Corps built a warming shelter there, under a U.S. Forest Service contract. Highway workers created a dirt road to the tow and the shelter.

Reportedly, the ski hill was moved down to its present location on the east side of the pass in 1955, and the old hill was lost. However, initially there was no parking at the new hill, so folks skied down Bunny Hop at the old hill from where their cars were parked and took the chair back up there at the end of the day.

CREEDE SKI HILL

A service club in Creede operated this hill, which was located southeast of the town (GPS coordinates 37°47'41"N, 106°51'32"W). The ski area opened in the '60s and ran through the decade, possibly into the early '70s, according to Kenny Wylie, who runs the Mines and Memories store in Creede and shared information and memories with the authors. Wylie said:

> [The] *Rotary Club started it, the Creede Rotary Club, and we think it was in 1964. Charles Steele owned the gas station here, and he rebuilt the motor in that old Chevy pickup and put duals on one side. And George Wince, who was the ranch manager at the La Garita Ranch…took a little D-4 cat and went over there and pulled that little pickup all the way to the top… and then they set the poles. And the Rotary Club bought the rope and they built that tow…We skied down there, everybody did, everybody went down there learned how to ski…and had a great time…All the Rotary Club wanted to do was pay for the gas. They had volunteers that'd keep it gassed up. That building…they built it, and somebody manned it. And they had a little propane bottle in there with a little gas stove, and they'd heat up hot chocolate and sell soda pop and hot dogs. And we all learned to ski there. I went in the navy in '69, and sometime in the '70s it dwindled—everybody lost enthusiasm for people to go and do the labor. I can't remember when they took down the towers…We had more fun down there…every Saturday and Sunday all winter long, clear up until the end of March, first of April—and if it snowed then, we'd go again.*[143]

Iris Birdsey also shared memories about the ski hill. There was one day when the rope tow wasn't working for some reason. A young man named

Randy McClure had "a snow machine" that would hold about six people, she said. He would take people up, and they would ski down. After a while, Randy wanted to ski, so Iris's husband, Rocky, told him, "Iris can drive the ski machine." And he was real skeptical, but Iris ended up driving it up and down the slope while everyone else skied. She remembered, "He was like in awe of my ability to drive that machine, like a women wasn't supposed to be able to do that."[144]

Some believe the hill was used informally before World War II and may have even had another rope tow during the 1950s.

17

San Juan County

Skiing High, Wild and Fast

A power line winds down the slope and skiers generally follow the route of the line.
The run is about three miles long and ends back at the highway at Mill Creek Lodge.
—Durango-Cortez (CO) Herald, *1966*[145]

T he county line between here is a straight line going east–west. It divides a lopsided triangle with some of the most beautiful country

Skiers make tracks on a hill close to Highway Camp. *Courtesy Animas Museum.*

in Colorado through which the Million Dollar Highway winds. The top of the triangle is San Juan County, and the bottom portion is La Plata County.

Silverton in San Juan County was relatively isolated. In the early days, people only stayed there when it was warm. Once they stayed all year, skis were their transportation in and out of the area during winter, allowing them to get supplies and mail and to visit other communities not served by the train.

Durango in La Plata County enjoyed milder winters, but the two communities shared a skiing legacy, and people in both counties have no doubt traveled between counties to ski. However, "the early ski hill locations in southern San Juan County were selected and used primarily by Durango/La Plata county people," according to Robert McDaniel, retired director of the Animas Museum in Durango.[146] McDaniel, other ski enthusiasts and newspapers told about skiing.

CASCADE SKI COURSES (CASCADE MEADOWS, JARVIS MEADOWS AND MILL CREEK)

Prior to completion of the highway over Coal Bank Pass, the road to Silverton from Durango followed a much longer and lower route called the Lime Creek Road. At that time, locals chose to ski on meadows near it and near Cascade Creek. Because of the many hills people skied, there has been some confusion as to the names and locations of them—the authors can only give approximate locations—but they were in the same vicinity, run by the same folks and centered on the junction of the old road and the new highway (GPS coordinates 37°39'31"N, 107°48'28"W).

Cascade Meadows was an area of open meadows on the north side of Cascade Creek, on the south flank of Engineer Mountain and uphill from a "highway camp" where people parked near the intersection. Folks created a rough lodge there, a three-sided shelter open to the south made of poles and tin. McDaniel described how people used this area and the first documented tow in La Plata County:

> *Bob Balliger told me that to get to that rope tow location (1937–1939, or so) they parked at the highway camp and hiked uphill. I recall him saying it wasn't a terribly long hike. The hill behind the highway camp*

Folks pose with skis at an early lodge. *Courtesy Animas Museum.*

is relatively steep and forested, however, so the tow wasn't really close to the camp—it was uphill some distance where the relatively gentle, open meadows are located.[147]

The *Durango Herald-Democrat* told its readers about preparations for this area in 1937. "All the machinery on the Cascade Ski Course will be in place by next Sunday. It is thought that the course will be completely ready for use by the first of the year."[148]

Less than a month earlier, the paper had reported that directors of the San Juan Basin Ski and Winter Sports Association had met at the power company office concerning the area:

Jack Lee, president of the organization, was authorized to proceed with the actual construction of the tow back and to co-operate with Louis Rist of the Forest Service to get the grounds in shape so skiing could commence with the first snow...The run will be officially known as the Cascade Ski Course.[149]

Fred Klatt (front) and friends work on tow at Cascade. *Courtesy Animas Museum.*

Fred Klatt (right) and William Crawley ski at Cascade. *Courtesy Animas Museum.*

Jarvis Meadows was south of Cascade Creek and consisted of smaller, open meadows in and near the current Cascade Village development. Patt Yeager Emmett said that some of the local skiers, including the Yeager family, installed and used a rope tow in this area, probably in the 1940s.

The *Durango Herald-Democrat* reported, "North of the city some 25 miles is one of the finest tows in the area, the Cascade Ski Tow, which is owned and operated by the Durango Ski Association."[150]

After the new highway was completed, a lodge was moved almost a mile up the hill and expanded. It was called the Mill Creek Lodge (see the next section on Coal Bank Pass) and was run privately. Emmett said that the Yeagers operated a tow on the slope across the highway from the new location of the shelter.

Coal Bank Pass

This area is located about thirty-two miles north of Durango on one of two high points on the way to Silverton. It was skied by residents of both communities and by others from the 1950s to the late '60s. Skiers would be dropped off at the top of the pass (GPS coordinates 37°41'52"N, 107°46'40"W) and ski down a power line cut and series of long meadows to a highway switchback down the south side (GPS coordinates 37°40'45"N, 107°47'36"W). This made for a run of over one and a half miles. Skiers could also continue another half mile and emerge at the highway across from the Mill Creek Lodge (GPS coordinates 37°40'23"N, 107°47'41"W).

Reese Miller reported on a conversation he had with Nancy Marsh, who was the daughter of Fred Brinker. Brinker lived in Durango for many years and regularly commuted to Silverton for his work as a mining engineer. Miller said:

> When the highway was relocated from Lime Creek to Coal Bank, he thought there was potential for a ski run such as the one from Berthoud Pass. His children, Tyler and Nancy, were both good skiers and pioneered the Coal Bank route. Coal Bank's "lift" was parents or friends shuttling skiers from Mill Creek to the top of the pass as many times as good nature would allow. Since the run consisted mostly of two tracks, there were a lot of knee injuries from tips getting hung up in the side of the track.[151]

McDaniel skied Coal Bank and wrote that there was no hiking necessary and folks could take multiple runs:

> It was a very popular ski trip in the 1950s and early 1960s before Purgatory was developed. The power line clearing was not very steep for

Patricia Colleen Yeager rides the rope tow on Mill Creek in 1947. *Courtesy of Patt Yeager Emmett.*

*skiing and a track was set in the powder that most skiers followed. Once it
got packed out to any degree, a skier could get going pretty fast since there
wasn't really any turning involved. To control your speed, you would have to*

*ski out into the powder—or crash! Since the exposure was basically south,
fresh snow would settle and get crusty pretty soon after the sun came out.
Long, sunny periods could make for some fairly treacherous snow conditions.
But we thought it was fun, and a lot of people did it.*[152]

A 2001 article in *Historic Durango* painted a good picture of skiing at
Coal Bank:

*Let's imagine several carloads of families and friends heading up Coal
Bank Pass north of Animas City. As they were driving up the West Animas
Road, singing and anticipating the day, did they realize they were pioneers?*

*The wagon- or car-load anticipated a day of schussing and fun to be
found as the snow boomed down from the summit of Coal Bank to the Mill
Creek Lodge... "We'll meet at Mill Creek Lodge to work out the shuttle..."*

*A day of skiing began. The route was a single smooth shining
track...Lunch [or] hot coffee was an event in the lodge.*[153]

Peter Bronski tells skiers how to backcountry ski there now in his book
Powder Ghost Towns. He writes that plans were in the works in the 1960s for
a ski area at the pass on Engineer Mountain, but the U.S. Forest Service
decided against issuing a permit. The area remained as it had always been.

VELOCITY PEAK

This unique ski track, which was dedicated to speed skiing in the 1980s, was
in the Storm Peak Basin north of Silverton (GPS coordinates 37°51'50"N,
107°38'40"W). The location was picked because of its elevation of over
twelve thousand feet, with the thin air reducing wind resistance; a steep,
even slope; and a good run out onto the frozen and snow-covered lake at the
bottom. It was a perfect location—except for the difficult access—for the
setting of world speed skiing records.

In April 1980, Kevin Spencer, reporting for the *Durango-Cortez (CO) Herald,*
wrote that the basin was groomed and awaiting a ski record. The setting
was as dramatic as the coming event: a speed skiing championship. "It's
surrounded by gigantic cliffs of the San Juan Mountains. The main event
is placed in the middle of what seems like a giant horseshoe, with towering
granite walls keeping in the competition."[154]

The Storm Peak skiing track was a fast ride. *Courtesy of Robert McDaniel.*

That first year, the American World Speed Skiing Championships was held Monday to Saturday in one week, with two speed skiing classifications: Standard Equipment, with maximum ski length of 223 centimeters, and Unlimited Class, with skis no longer than 240 centimeters.

Spencer wrote that expectations were high that the North American speed record of 93.143 miles per hour (mph) would be shattered, and the world speed record of 124.04 mph would also go down.[155]

Spectators came to the event, for which admission was five dollars per day. They parked in Silverton for three dollars and took buses from the Grand

Imperial Hotel in Silverton to the road's end, about one and a half miles from the finish area in the basin. Spectators would have to walk or cross country the rest of the way.

Speed skiers spent the Saturday before the competition boot and ski packing the course and taking practice runs. "The speed demons started their runs only halfway up the steep course, which is 11,300 feet at the bottom and 13,000 feet at the top...The highest speed reached for the day was 84 mph."[156]

Another newspaper article gave more details about the hill, reporting that it had a vertical drop of 1,300 feet. "The first 1,000 feet of the course starts out at degrees of 51, 45, 22, 28 and 21. The final 1,000 feet, the outrun, is at 27 and 30 degrees gradient."[157]

Kalevi Hakkinen was the chief of the course at Storm Peak Basin and a racer. He was the World Champion Speed Skier in 1968.

Steve McKinney, a speed skier who set the world record in 1979 in Portillo, Chile, was credited with bringing the championship to the United States and Silverton. He told Spencer, "This is what we have been waiting for a long time. We are bringing it all home."[158]

A week after the competition, Spencer reported that Franz Weber had the fastest time of the week, at 117.34 mph, to win the World Speed Skiing Championship and established the hill record. There was a three-way tie for second place; "coming in at 184.71 kmph, or 114.52 mph, were Bob Miller, Paul Buschmann and Alain Stump."[159] Weber broke the record two more times before the hill was lost.

Storm Peak, Inc. (Jim Jackson, Paul Dunn and B.J. Lenihan) put on the competition. It had planned on installing a lift to take competitors up the hill to the course; however, that wasn't feasible, so it took them up on a snowcat to the middle of the course, and they had to walk up the rest of the way. This cut down on the practice runs for racers. This group had financial difficulties and was bypassed by the International Speed Skiing Association in 1982; the Silverton Chamber of Commerce organized the event that year, and Tamarron resort provided housing and transportation.

That year, a woman who lived in Telluride named Marti Martin-Kuntz earned a women's world record time of about 111.29 mph. In a video profile for the Telluride Historical Museum, she said that she had raced different types of courses and then someone told her that her build was right for speed skiing. "And at that point I think I was really ready...and kind of felt like I'd like to go faster."[160]

The hill's life was short; promoters decided to move to Arapahoe Basin for the 1983 competition, saying that the Silverton site was too difficult, logistically. However, its life was distinguished, and the subpeak in the basin where the race was held was renamed Velocity Peak.

Jim Jackson wouldn't let the competition at this site go, however. He worked for eight years to bring the championships back to Velocity Peak, and in 1991, he made it happen. After that, the hill seems to have been lost to racing.

18

La Plata County

Tough Guys, Rope Tows and Local Hills

Comes snow and the cold weather sports enthusiast can have his fling in the San Juan Basin.
—Durango Herald-Democrat, *1951*[161]

La Plata County is home to Durango, the largest town in southwest Colorado and regional hub of arts and culture. Between it and Silverton, in neighboring San Juan County, runs the famous Durango & Silverton Railroad. The counties also share great skiing and ski areas.

Robert McDaniel spoke with the authors about skiing in the county, and Patt Yeager Emmett told them about the hills and the tows. They painted a picture of beloved local hills and history.

Skiing started here as it did in so many parts of Colorado: people got around on Norwegian snowshoes using one long pole. In the 1870s, miners were probably skiing, according to McDaniel, and folks were skiing to deliver the mail. "Hans Aspaas and others carried the mail from Silverton to Del Norte or wherever. Helen Ruth Aspaas said that Hans Sr. was carrying the mail with skis the first winter they were there. People didn't winter over in Silverton the first few years. But, from the time they stayed there year-round, they skied in and out."[162]

In the 1920s, friends skied for fun at Animas City (now the north part of Durango). McDaniel said, "Up in the north part of town, there are some glacial moraines from the Animas Glacier that came down the valley... People from both Animas City and Durango skied down those moraines at least as early as the 1920s. Several families were very involved in skiing in La Plata County, but none so much as the Yeager family. Various members of that family were involved in one way or another with most of the early ski hills. Attorney Reese Miller remembered them. "The Yeagers were back country skiers without peer…They all were masters of the telemark turn and skied in the trees and back country as much as on designated areas. Also, they were probably responsible for some of the early rope tows in the area."[163] McDaniel agreed:

> *The Yeagers were, I think, widely considered to be the best skiers around here in the early days. They were mountain men, they were loggers, they were miners, they were your basic all-around tough guys—and gals. There are some great stories about the Yeagers doing…rescues of avalanche victims in the La Plata Mountains…These guys kind of had their own tows.*

Barney Yeager Sr. had two sons, Barney Jr. and Ronnie. Ronnie went to the '72 and '76 Olympics on the cross-country team, and his older brother, Barney Jr., was state champion in the high school circuit. Patt Yeager Emmett said that Barney Sr. set up tows in different places.

Competition didn't really come to Durango until the 1950s, when Dolph Kuss came to town, organized and coached a local junior ski team. Before that, the hardworking locals in Durango and the surrounding area created ski hills that ran for a few, fun years (sometimes people in other areas referred to it as Engineer Mountain skiing). They also created longer-running areas that have provided fun for decades and still do. Winter carnivals also drew skiers beginning in the 1950s. Durango's long-running winter celebration Snowdown started in 1979 and is still going strong.

CHIPMUNK HILL

This area had many names, including Lechner Field. The ski hill was actually in a meadow below Highway 550 about eighteen miles north of Durango (GPS coordinates 37°32'44"N, 107°49'24"W).

McDaniel passed on information to the authors from Charlie Langdon's *Durango Ski*; specifically, he sent firsthand accounts of the tow at Chipmunk Hill.

Walt (left) and Bob Balliger wait with skis atop their car at Chipmunk Hill. *Courtesy Animas Museum.*

A boy jumps at Chapman Hill, the town hill in Durango. *Courtesy Animas Museum.*

In the book, Nick Turner said, "There used to be a little ski area there above Lechners' called Chipmunk Hill. Jack Lee, Walt Balliger and my father put an old Model A engine at the bottom of the hill. It was hooked up to a quarter-inch cable; no safety gates or anything. It was like a rope tow, but it was steel cable, and it tore up the gloves and everything else…the lift at Chipmunk Hill was there for three or four years."

McDaniel said, "They moved the tow from Cascade Meadows [see the San Juan County section] down to Chipmunk Hill…it's right by the highway. We used to go toboggan there when I was a kid."[164] The tow from Chipmunk Hill was moved to Chapman Hill during World War II. At that time, everyone knew it as Third Avenue Hill, and later, it was called Calico Hill. They may have moved the tow there because of gas rationing.

Langdon confirms that account. He writes, "The splintery, glove-chewing rope tow remained at Third Avenue…from wartime until 1954."[165]

The hill in town was eventually named for Colton Chapman, a mover and shaker who did a lot of the work along with volunteers from the ski club.

Columbine Guest Ranch

In 1947, the *Durango Herald-Democrat* reported, "The ski course is located east of the ranch headquarters at the north end of Columbine [L]ake."[166] The exact location is unclear, but a short open slope facing the entrance to the ranch seemed to be the most logical location for a ski hill (GPS coordinates 37°37'4"N, 107°48'34"W).

The *Durango Herald-Democrat* told its readers about skiing here in 1951. "Some of the finest skiing in the state can be had at the Columbine Guest Ranch tow."[167]

Reese Miller of Durango told about another tow in the vicinity. "There was a rope tow just south of Durango Mountain Resort on the west side of the highway."[168] This was where he got tangled up in the rope tow and would have been killed in the bull wheel except for the quick thinking on the part of Dick Yeager.

McDaniel clarified that this tow was somewhere in the vicinity of a seventy-meter jump hill that was built about 1970. "As he says, it was west of the highway, and it would have been across the highway from the Columbine Guest Ranch and slightly north."[169]

Cowboy Hill

The *Durango Herald-Democrat* wrote, "There was even a rope tow west of Durango on the Yeager Ranch, a place nicknamed 'Cowboy Hill,' in the late 1950s."[170]

Cowboy Hill was about five miles west of Durango, right by the highway. Coloradoskihistory.com reports that the area was between mile markers 77 and 78 on U.S. Highway 160 (GPS coordinates 37°15'53"N, 107°57'49"W).[171] It had one rope tow powered "by a flathead Ford V8" and two runs. It was open from 1957 to 1959.

John McMillan listed it as being "on Hesperus Hill but not the site of current Hesperus area" and reported that it was the last of Yeager's tows and was abandoned after someone stole his rope, possibly three times.[172]

The remnants of a roller packer remain at the site.

Tamarron

This area was located at the Tamarron Resort north of Durango (GPS coordinates 37°30'3"N, 107°48'44"W). A ski area guide from 1976 read, "Tamarron is a PRIVATE SKI AREA with a beginning slope for the convenience of resort guests. Sunshine 80% of season; annual snowfall 48 inches."[173] However, the snowfall total was probably off; Purgatory's average annual snowfall is well over two hundred inches and it's only about ten miles north of Tamarron, according to McDaniel.

The area ran from November to April, from 9:00 a.m. to 4:00 p.m. daily. It had one slope, one rope tow and a drop of fifty vertical feet. Ten part-time instructors worked there under Fritz Tatzer, the ski school director.

The *Durango-Cortez (CO) Herald* reported on the area:

> *Tamarron Resort has started construction on a new novice ski area to be completed for the 1981–82 winter ski season beginning Nov. 15, 1981.*
>
> *Highlighting the new area will be the most up-to-date snow making equipment, insuring a full season of the very best conditions. Additionally, the area will be fully lighted, providing the exciting new dimension of night skiing.*
>
> *Lift capabilities will feature a new Horvig double chair lift, which along with the existing rope tow will handle 1,000 skiers per hour and will*

*provide Tamarron with the best and most complete capabilities in the area
for the beginning skier.*

*Tamarron management feels the new facilities will enable them to provide an
outstanding beginners' program. Rounding out the total Tamarron ski experience
is the availability of complete instruction, an extensive cross-country program
and trail grid, and both Alpine and Nordic equipment rental facilities.*[174]

The ski area did not last long. Resort management decided to send guests to
Purgatory for skiing.

FOREST LAKES

This area was located in a subdivision called Forest Lakes, north of Bayfield
off County Road 501 (GPS coordinates 37°19'16"N, 107°35'28"W) and was
built for the residents of the subdivision.

Coloradoskihistory.com reports that the area operated from 1972 to 1983,
from November to April each year. Tickets were eight dollars for adults and
five dollars for children. The area had a Poma lift as well as a J-bar for
beginning skiers and riders.

A concrete block for the lift remains at the left on the Forest Lakes hill. *Peter Boddie photo.*

Ron Dunavant skied there in the 1970s; in fact, he learned to ski there. He said, "You skied up hill." Bayfield schools took kids up there, and for one dollar per day, they'd ski a half-day after lunch. The area had an eight-sided lodge.[175]

Montezuma County

Two Hills, Two Ski Clubs

Skiing is a fine sport because families can join in outings together, regardless of skill. One sees youngsters less than 10 years old both at Stoner and Mill Creek who are as good or better than their parents.
—Arthurt Ballantine Jr., 1955[176]

This county is in the Four Corners area; that is, it includes the geographic point where Colorado, New Mexico, Arizona and Utah meet. Northeast of the biggest town in the county, Cortez, is a ski area that has served the folks here for decades.

Outside the town of Mancos, there was a hill that ran for a much shorter time. However, it was also built with the sweat equity of volunteers who wanted to ski.

The newspaper in Durango, which kept changing its name before the Ballantine family published it, reported on both hills and clubs, repeatedly.

MANCOS HILL SKI COURSE

Mancos Hill refers to the high point east of Mancos on U.S. Highway 160 after a long climb from either direction; it also marks the dividing line between Montezuma and La Plata Counties and was the site of a small ski hill located just off of the highway to the south (GPS coordinates

37°19'56"N, 108°12'31"W). The newspaper in Durango reported on this hill in 1947:

> *Mancos Hill Ski Club is ready to go at their Mancos [Hill] course. A rope tow has been installed and will be in operation Sundays only. The course, which is open to the public, will be in operation as soon as snow conditions are right, Earl Erickson, a member of the board, said yesterday. Jack Allum is president of the Mancos group.*

John Allum, Jack's son, wrote down his memories of the ski course in 2007. He said that the U.S. Forest Service, led by Earl Erickson, built a cabin on top of the hill. There, his mom, Nellie Allum, sold tickets, donuts and hot chocolate. Skiers warmed up at a big fireplace. "The foundation of the cabin is still in place on Mancos Hill but the cabin was moved to the corner of County Road L and Forest Service Road F567."[177]

The club—which included Russell Culp, Clay Bader, Emory Lovett, Milton Roberts and others—built the course and cleared the oak brush from it by hand. They mounted an old 1928 Chevy pickup on a platform of cedar posts that was six feet high at the top of the hill so the weight of the rope would keep the tension on the drive wheel. "The Forest Service bought a rope about 800 feet long and an inch in diameter and the two ends of the rope were spliced together so that it made a circle. The rope was looped over a tire rim mounted on the right rear axel of the pickup. Tall posts with wheel rims mounted about 8 feet off the ground and spaced about every 10 yards down the hill were used to carry the rope back down the hill. A big wheel (probably from something like a rear tractor tire rim) was located at [the] bottom of the hill with a yoke to hold the hub. The yoke was then tied… with a 'block and tackle'…to a large 'corner' post so that the rope could be tightened."[178]

Jack Allum would carry a five-gallon can of gas and a five-gallon can of water to the top of the hill to start the pickup. He wrote:

> *Once it was warmed up, he would [put] the transmission in the lowest gear possible (we called it compound) and the rope would start moving. To use the tow you picked up the rope with your right hand and let it slide through the palm of your hand (you really needed good leather gloves). Then you would slowly tighten your grip and away you would go up the hill pulled by the rope. Tow ropes had a tendency to twist, so it was fairly easy to get a coat, glove, or scarf wrapped up in the rope so that you could not get off*

when you wanted [to]. *So a safety switch was created by draping a wire
between two posts at the top of the run in line with the rope. The wire was
an extension of the coil wire (the wire from the coil to the distributor) on the
engine. So, if someone got hung up in the rope, they would break the wire
as they went between the posts and that would stop the spark going to the
engine and the engine would stop.*[179]

For the first two years, the Mancos Hill Ski Club charged fifty cents a day
or two dollars for a family season pass and operated on weekends. When
the U.S. Forest Service insisted that it carry insurance, the club had to raise
prices to one dollar per day or six dollars for a family season pass. Skiers
packed snow by sidestepping uphill and had to fill in sitzmarks after falls.
John Allum wrote:

*Dad eventually built a packer that consisted of two big wheels (probably
off of a buck rake or wheat drill) and bolted 2x4's around the outside of
the rim. Then he built a yoke from the axles so that it had a handle to hang
on to. Once the rope tow was moving, one of the men would pull the packer
to the top of the hill and then ski down with it to help pack the snow.*[180]

The hill operated for several years and was listed in the 1951 Christmas
issue of *Colorado Wonderland*:

*Located Mancos Hill, San Juan Nat'l Forest. Elev.: 8,000 feet. Season:
Jan. 1 to April 1. Reached Via: U.S. 160, 8 mi. from Mancos, 22 mi.
from Durango. Runs: One, 1,350 ft., 150-ft. drop. Tows: Rope, 1,000
ft., 250-foot rise.*

A sports column talked about it in 1958, a year when snow seems to have
been insufficient in the entire basin:

*At Mancos, where the Mancos Ski Club has installed new safety devices
on its 600-foot rope tow, there is insufficient snow for skiing according to
Earl Erickson.*

*When the snow is good, the tow on the western crest of Mancos Hill is
usually open Sunday afternoons. The area is one of the best in the Basin
for children. Refreshments are sold by club members.*[181]

STONER

This ski area was a "going concern," as Robert McDaniel told the authors. It operated for thirty-four years. The hill is off Colorado Highway 145 at Stoner (GPS coordinates 37°35'2"N, 108°19'14"W), northeast of Cortez. The base area for Stoner is on private property, but the ski slopes and the cut for the lift are clearly visible from the highway. The ski lodge at the base of the slope has been converted into a private home.

An editorial written by the owner and publisher of the *Durango Herald*, Arthur Ballantine Jr., tells the story of the first couple of years:

> *The enlarged ski area at Stoner is an excellent example of what a determined community can accomplish.*
>
> *The Ski-Hi Ski [C]lub, a group of younger marrieds from Cortez, first put into shape one hill by working summer weekends to remove the stumps and brush. Then they started on a larger project of putting an adjacent 3,000-foot run into shape and investing $30,000 in a T-bar tow.*
>
> *Merwyn Akins of Dolores had confidence in the club and built a handsome, comfortable lodge which has been open for the last year. The result is a fine, new skiing area which adds to the recreational facilities of the Basin.*
>
> *On Sunday, January 16th, the new T-bar tow will be dedicated. Mere snow is all that is needed to make the occasion a complete success. While*

The Stoner Ski Area has not changed too much since its glory days. *Peter Boddie photo.*

there was enough snow on the rope tow hill to give everyone a good time last weekend, the new hill needs a deeper snow base. President McNeill and the other club members were able to move most of the big obstructions last summer but some of the smaller ones remain...

While the Basin may never attract as many outside skiers as Aspen and Sun Valley due to distance, there is a big local demand particularly if skiing instruction for children is developed. New Mexico cars flock into the Basin every weekend and a number of parties come from Texas. Skiing crowds are usually good crowds to have in your midst.

Stoner is adding splendid, new skiing facilities amid pleasant surroundings... The future for Basin skiing [looks] good.[182]

A ski guide from 1957 listed Stoner's particulars:

Stoner Ski Area, 420 miles from Denver, reached via Highway 145, north of Cortez 28 miles or 16 miles from Dolores in San Juan National Forest. Area offers open trails and runs for beginners and expert skiers; 3,000 ft., 1,000 ft. drop; 3,500 ft., 1,050 drop; 1,500 ft., 400 ft. drop; 1,700 ft., 400 ft. drop. New slalom 1,300 ft. long, 400 ft. drop. Rates: All lifts all day, adults $2.75; children $1.75; rope tow only, adults $1.75, children $1.50; single ride 50¢. Large warming shelter available. A new lodge at foot of course accommodates 65, has complete facilities. Cabins at Stoner and hotel and court facilities in Cortez and Dolores. Volunteer ski patrol supervises trails. Season—December to April, open weekends and holidays. Operated by [Ski-Hi] Ski Club, Inc., Cortez, Colorado.[183]

Fifteen years into the ski area's existence, the newspaper covered the area again, this time for its "See & Ski Southwestern Colorado" supplement:

The Stoner course, now in its [15th] year of operation, offers an abundance of skiing experiences for the sportsmen of all ages and abilities.

With a vertical drop of 1,000 feet, the skier has a choice of four major runs and a variety of trails. Two runs are 3,000 feet in length and two of them are 1,500 feet in length. The area is served by a 1,000-foot rope tow and a Constam T-Bar which extends up the mountain 3,000 feet. And, of course, a bunny slope with a private rope!

The ski club continues to add to and improve the slopes. This year a project was undertaken by the [Ski]-Hi skiers to widen the popular Akin Run which drops sharply to the left of the T-Bar. Having been steep and

*narrow, it is now tripled in width. A road was also completed to the top
of the tow this summer....Since those early days of few skiers and little
interest, the* [Ski]-*Hi Ski Club has come a long way. Not only has the local
population come to think "skiing," but, also, Stoner continues to attract
many outsiders. With increased ski facilities and increased skiers, it looks
like the sport is here in the Four Corners to stay.*[184]

It was listed in at least two editions of *The White Book of US Ski Areas*. In
1984, credit cards were being accepted, there were four instructors, Dick
Gallant was the ski instructor, the vertical rise was listed as 1,250 feet and
a unique price structure had been put in place: "Rates: Start at $9.00 at 10
a.m. & drop $.50 every ½ hr 'til it's free! Student & ski club members rate is
$1 less than rate is at the time."[185]

Coloradoskihistory.com reports that the area closed in 1985 when a T-bar
tower fell over. Reese Miller said, "There was a fatality there related to the
bull wheel at the top of the hill. The run was a steep swath cut straight down
the side of the canyon."[186]

20

San Miguel County

Skiing Everywhere and a Portable Rope Tow

Since the weather man has hit us amidships with a real winter storm, we can forget about baseball for a time and possibly devote our attention to a ski tournament.
—Telluride Daily Journal, *1923*[187]

This county has been about mining—and skiing—as much as or more than any county in Colorado.

Bill "Senior" Mahoney was from a longtime mining family and became a shift boss in the Idarado Mine. He was also from a skiing family. In fact, the skis his granddad made and skied on in the 1890s at Bonanza, Colorado—where Mahoney was born—are on display at the Telluride Historical Museum.

His family moved to Telluride in 1931, when he was three, and he and his brothers started skiing then. Mahoney spent time with the authors talking about skiing and sharing what he knew about lost areas. The quotes in this section are from that interview except where noted differently; he is also featured in a documentary produced by the museum.[188]

Skiing started with merely getting around on skis here, too; one rancher who lived on Horsefly Mesa, Simon Hellman, made a long trip to Telluride to do business and then had to go home the way he came; he "was forced to make an 18-mile trip on snowshoes to get to Leonard and catch a train to Telluride."[189]

Later, a small number of residents became interested in skiing for recreation. These were miners and their family members. Others from different areas of the county, and with different occupations, joined in.

In 1923, a famous skier visited Telluride and advised folks:

> *That Telluride should have a ski club and that conditions here are ideal for several months of the finest winter sport imaginable, is the opinion of Lars Haugen, champion ski jumper of America. Mr. Haugen was a visitor in Telluride on Saturday and is enthusiastic about skiing conditions in this section. He is a booster for skiing and believes that Telluride should have a real live active ski club that might in the course of a year or two promote a ski tournament which would attract as much attention as the now famous Steamboat Springs tournament which is held each year.*[190]

Meanwhile, the kids skied Catholic Hill in Telluride (where the Catholic church was). Then, they moved on to skijoring behind cars on the streets. As they got older, they skied Grizzly Gulch down from the Alta Mine through the trees, down Boomerang Road to the valley floor or following a power line route into the Prospect Basin and up again and down to town.

Folks ski at Grizzly Gulch. *Courtesy of Senior Mahoney.*

Later, they would ride a snowmobile or snow machines to the high peaks, hike up even higher and ski the bowls, sometimes skiing across rocks and grass to get to other patches of snow. They were careful about avalanche danger but had some lucky breaks for sure. One really dangerous place they skied when they were older was called the Mammoth Slide. Those who went with them got to ski in these majestic places too—and got to drive the snow machines up steep hills.

Different people kept coming to Telluride and getting hooked on the town and the skiing. Teacher Bruce Palmer wanted to show people a new type of skiing—skiing with turns. Those who came later wanted to harness the energy of the skiers and make a large ski resort.

The passion of these men and the local skiers paid off for the many when, as Telluride was dying as a mining town, it embraced skiing. The local hills went by the wayside, but they were not forgotten.

Lizard Head Pass

In the 1920s, the Telluride Ski Club would take the train up to Lizard Head Pass between Dolores and Telluride, according to Mahoney.

The Rio Grande and Southern Railroad maintained regular service over the pass to the mines until the late '40s. In 1924 and '25, locals would ride the train to go skiing; the train would drop people off and pick them up later, or they could spend the night at the depot, which "was a sophisticated place." People would walk up into the trees and ski the open slopes on the Black Face (GPS coordinates 37°48'47"N, 107°54'24"W).

Years later, the Galloping Goose carried people over the rails and over Lizard Head Pass to Dolores until about 1952 or '53. Mahoney said, "I've got some pictures of me and the wife riding in it. She lived in Rico before I married her, and when she went to high school, she'd have to ride the Galloping Goose, and she rode it for four years." Unfortunately, when she tried to be a skier, she broke her leg. And that was the end of it, he said.

Around 1946, folks used a portable rope tow on Lizard Head Pass. When the servicemen came back after the war, Mahoney's brother, Bob, put up the rope tow there. "He was an avid skier, and he would take the lead."

Bob and the guys created the tow themselves. "You'd have a rope that made a loop, take it double, wrap it around the spare tire and take the

The Telluride Ski Club takes a break for a group photo. *Courtesy of Senior Mahoney.*

The Galloping Goose transported skiers to the hills in the first half of the twentieth century, running between Ridgeway and Dolores. *Peter Boddie photo.*

tire off of it and then put a shive block up in around a tree and, if the rope dragged, you had to hold the rope from dragging in the snow. But it worked."

Firecracker Hill (and Other Telluride Town Hills)

"We built ten rope tows in Telluride during my time," Mahoney said. "We had a 1929 or 1927 Nash car. It was our portable rope tow. We had a long rope, and we would take it and put a shive block on the mountain or up on the hill. We spent more time setting it up than we did skiing."[191]

Firecracker Hill was the first or second one to have a tow, and it was located at what is now the town ballpark on the southeast side of Telluride (GPS coordinates 37°55'57"N, 107°48'27"W). You can see the small slope at the end of the park that is still used for sledding and tobogganing. Bob Mahoney and Ed Goldsworthy built it in 1944 or '46. The rope tow was moved around to several places on the south side of town, including some that are now part of runs at Telluride Ski Resort.

A few skiers spend a day on Firecracker Hill. *Courtesy of Senior Mahoney.*

Mahoney said that Tony Thornton and Gus Sands built a rope tow over at the beaver ponds downtown with a "Bratt Stratton" engine.

Thornton and Sands also set up a rope tow at Grizzly Gulch in an area cleared for a new development in power. "Telluride was where they generated power first in the United States, matter of fact—maybe in the world, I don't know…They had a twelve-thousand-volt power line coming down there…It was pretty narrow, and then we widened it out."

There was also a hill called Broomtail on the mesa where the mountain village is now. Bob Mahoney named it for the wild horses that were running there at one time.

SKYLINE RANCH

There was another ski area near Cushman Lake, along the road up to Lizard Head Pass, about halfway between Telluride and the turn off to Ophir, according to Mahoney. "The Goldsworthys owned it, and then it ended up being the Skyline Guest Ranch. And they had a rope tow off of an old portable tow there… let some of the young guys ski it." It was located off the Turkey Creek Mesa on the far end, the south end in the late 1940s or early '50s. The authors were not able to pinpoint the exact spot but have picked a logical location on an open slope at the south end of the lake (GPS coordinates 37°53'37"N, 107°53'15"W).

SKI DALLAS

This area was located on Colorado Highway 62, west of Ridgway at Sams, about four miles down from Dallas Divide on the west side (GPS coordinates 38°6'13"N, 107°57'25"W). An article in the 1966 supplement to the *Durango-Cortez (CO) Herald*, before the third year of operation for Ski Dallas, gave details:

> *Ski Dallas is the result of three skiing families who devoted a lot of time and work to give the area what they considered a much-needed family recreation area. The area reopened with improved facilities in December of 1964 and has continued to improve and grow ever since.*

160

The Ski Dallas run is still visible. *Peter Boddie photo.*

Ski Dallas is looking forward to its third season this winter with improved trails, better grooming and a challenging new trail ready. The area, with a vertical rise of 800 feet on two main trails (one for beginners and one for intermediate and experts), is served by a 2,100-foot T-Bar lift with a capacity of 400 skiers per hour.

Facilities at the base area include a warming house and a snack bar. A ski school is also available with Jerry Peasman as the certified instructor... The area, which is open on weekends and holidays only, has rates of $7.50 for families, $2 for adults, $1.50 for students from 10 to 18 years of age, $1 for children under 10. These are full day rates as the area does not offer half-day rates.[192]

Its years of operation were 1962 to 1976. Coloradoskihistory.com has posted good memories from people who worked at and skied the area. They share tidbits, like the fact that there was only night skiing there when there was a full moon; some years, there was so much snow that it had to be scooped below the T-bar; the area held Dallas Daze at the end of each season with fun events; and local families could work to ski by doing various jobs. Carla A. wrote, "It was a lot of work but a great experience for all of us. We have a hard time driving by the area now and see[ing] the trees growing up on the runs and the lodge becoming part of the new house that was built in the old parking lot."[193]

21

Ouray County

Skiing Miners, Danger and Disappointment

Electric power will be supplied for the ski tow at Ohio Park for the San Juan Ski Club of Ouray, Colo.
—Steamboat Pilot, *1938*[194]

Bill "Senior" Mahoney also told about skiing in this county, where mining was once the economic engine. He said he had a picture of four or five women with long skirts skiing up at the Catbird Mine above Ouray.[195]

Tourists come to see the spectacular peaks and cliffs, meadows and vistas around the towns of Ridgway and Ouray, mostly in the summer, but there has been a lot of skiing here, as well as attempts to create resorts.

Avalanches have always been a danger in Ouray County; Mahoney said that many miners were killed in them. He added, "In the state of Colorado, around Silverton, Ouray and Telluride, the San Juan Mountains are the worst place for avalanches in the state—heck, maybe in the nation—because of the snow conditions."[196]

It's no wonder the townspeople in Ouray chose to make a ski hill in town on the valley floor for their children. However, adults did ski high up.

IRONTON PARK

This area was located up the Colorado Highway 550, south of Ouray in Ironton Park, a broad valley reached after a long steep climb from Ouray. The ski area was located near the north end of the park, close to a large lodge, the foundation of which is standing alongside the highway. The authors were not certain of the exact ski slope location but assumed it was in the open meadow area just north of the lodge (GPS coordinates 37°57'40"N, 107°39'41"W).

A weathered wheel from Ironton stands in Ouray. *Peter Boddie photo.*

A caption on a photograph from the Ouray County Historical Society, which Jack Clark Sr. sent to the authors, told a sad story:

Ski Lodge at Ironton Park. Partners Ralph Kullerstand and Joe Condotti built this lodge in the 1930s. Their enterprise included enhancing Crystal Lake and erecting a ski lift. The bricks came from the smokestack of the Saratoga Smelter. The two partners had a falling out, and they never opened for business. The St. Germain Foundation (the "I Am" religion) bought the site in the 1940s. The building burned, but the stone basement still sits along the highway.[197]

However, according to Clark, the ski lift did operate, at least for a short period. He said, "My uncle was Joe Condotti. When I was a boy, I used to run the ski hoist for the lift so my uncle could grease the pulleys. The ski lift was a seven-chair lift."[198]

Although nothing of the ski lift apparently remains in Ironton Park, you can see a small bull wheel gear from the lift at the northeast corner of Colorado Highway 550 and Ninth Street in Ouray.

DALLAS DIVIDE

Mahoney, who skied this area a time or two, said that there were two Dallas Divide ski areas. This one, the older one, was on the very top of Dallas Divide. The other was Ski Dallas (see the San Miguel County section).

People were apparently skiing at Dallas Divide in the 1930s and perhaps earlier, before any rope tow was installed. They skied the open slopes and aspen areas to the south of the highway and railroad tracks. As with Lizard Head Pass, some may have even ridden the train up from Ridgeway or from the Telluride side. Later on, a rope tow was added. We were uncertain of the exact location of the lift and ski slopes, but people could have skied anywhere along the north-facing slope at the top of the divide, just into Ouray County (GPS coordinates 38°5'40"N, 107°53'24"W).

Mahoney said, "The one on top of the Dallas Divide…created by a couple of guys from the Tenth Mountain Division…was right on the very top. It was just a kind of a steep hill there. They cut the quakees on it and put a rope tow up there and ran it off an old Jeep that the guys brought home

The Galloping Goose waits for passengers at Dallas Divide. *Courtesy of Senior Mahoney.*

Bruce Palmer jumps a barbed wire fence at Dallas Divide in 1938. *Courtesy of Senior Mahoney.*

from the service…In 1948, they built that." The tow ran only for a couple of years and then was moved to the Ski Dallas location.

A 1966 article tells about the change:

> *A few years ago one mail carrier, one assistant forest ranger and a cattle rancher, with enthusiasm as their prime asset, decided they could replace the old rope tow on the Dallas Divide ski area with a T-Bar lift. The group lacked just about everything except enthusiasm, including heavy equipment, but they demonstrated once again that the wheel and the lever can still function well.*[199]

Notes

INTRODUCTION

1. Davey, "Snow Dust."
2. Reese Miller, e-mail to Patt Emmett.
3. WNU Features, "Full Flight: Winter Sports Areas."
4. Coleman, *Ski Style*.
5. Bill Fetcher, e-mail to Caryn Boddie.
6. Reese Miller, e-mail to Patt Emmett.
7. National Ski Patrol, *Ski Patrol Manual*.
8. Colorado Ski and Snowboard Museum, "1972–76 Winter Olympics."

CHAPTER 1

9. *Summit County Journal*, "Breckenridge Should Capitalize Its Snowbanks."
10. Ibid., "Ski Course Put in Fine Condition."
11. Ibid., "Ski-Riding Now in Vogue."
12. Gilliland, *Summit*, 446.
13. Ibid., 444.
14. Hafnor, *Strange but True*.
15. *Summit County Journal*, "Why the Dillon Ski Course."
16. Ibid., "New Breckenridge Ski Course."
17. Ibid., "Ski Tournaments Are General Order."
18. Ibid., "Local Boys Make Good Ski Records."

19. Ibid., "Lower Blue River Boys."
20. Colorado Ski History website.
21. Colorado Wonderland, Inc., "Skiing Centers of Colorado."
22. Summit Historical, "Hoosier Pass Cabin."
23. Ibid.
24. Colorado Ski History website.

CHAPTER 2

25. Colorado Ski History website.
26. Coleman, *Ski Style*, 104.
27. *Estes Park Trail*, "Colorado in Paragraphs."
28. Colorado Ski Information Center, *Manual of Colorado Skiing*, 1957–58.
29. Brookshire, interview with the authors.
30. *Steamboat Pilot*, "New Ski School Opening at Climax."
31. Ibid.
32. Brookshire, interview with the authors.

CHAPTER 3

33. *Eagle Valley Enterprise*, "Ski Lift Is Near Completion."
34. Ibid., "Out Door Sports Club Organized in Eagle."
35. Ibid., "Ski Lift Is Near Completion."
36. Heicher, "Skiing Eagle."
37. Colorado Ski History website.
38. Colorado Visitors Bureau information.
39. Bronski, *Powder Ghost Towns*, 182–187.
40. Colorado Ski History website.
41. Wolf, "K Men Ready for Cooper Hill Test."

CHAPTER 4

42. Hauk, "Montezuma."
43. Willoughby, "Skiing Comes to Aspen."
44. Ibid.
45. Gardner-Smith, "Aspen Pioneer Roch Dies at 96." Also see Peter Shelton's *Aspen Skiing: The First Fifty Years*.
46. Willoughby, "Skiing Comes to Aspen."

47. Hayes, interview with the authors.
48. Hauk, "Montezuma."

CHAPTER 5

49. *Glenwood Post,* "New Ski Course Location Is Given to City."
50. *Steamboat Pilot,* "News of Our Neighbors," November 10, 1938.
51. *Glenwood Post,* "Skiing Conditions on Red Mountain are Excellent."
52. Ibid.
53. *Glenwood Post,* "New Ski Course Location Is Given to City."
54. Soncarty, "Red Mountain Helped Pioneer Western Skiing."
55. *Glenwood Post,* "Free Barbecue Will Be Oct. 26 at Red Mountain."
56. Soncarty, "Red Mountain Helped Pioneer Western Skiing."
57. Ibid.
58. Ibid.
59. Ibid.
60. Inter-Ski Services, *White Book of US Ski Areas.*

CHAPTER 6

61. *Steamboat Pilot,* "Northwestern Colorado."
62. Ibid., "Pagoda Woman Takes Census."
63. Ibid., "News of Our Neighbors," December 3, 1936.
64. Ibid., "News of Our Neighbors," September 4, 1947.
65. Ibid., "News of Our Neighbors," January 5, 1950.
66. Colorado Ski History website.

CHAPTER 7

67. *Steamboat Pilot,* "Skiers Marooned in Shelter Cabin."
68. *Aspen Daily Times,* "Get Out Your [Skis] and Take This In."
69. Fay, *Ski Tracks in the Rockies.*
70. *Steamboat Pilot,* "Winter Sports in Many Sections Gaining Momentum."
71. Colorado Ski Information Center, *Manual of Colorado Skiing,* 1957–58.
72. Ibid., 1962–63.
73. Colorado Visitors Bureau information.
74. Colorado Ski History website.

CHAPTER 8

75. *Steamboat Pilot*, "Northwestern Colorado."
76. *Aspen Daily Times*, "Delta Ski Fans Plan Unique Party."
77. Brewer, "Five More Lost Ski Areas."
78. Ibid.
79. Scott, *Coincidence? I Don't Think So*.
80. Colorado Wonderland, Inc., "Skiing Centers of Colorado."
81. Burritt, interview with Peter Boddie.
82. Kawamura, "Winter Recreation Area Operates on Mesa."

CHAPTER 9

83. Davey, "Snow Dust."
84. Brandt, "Cerro Summit," Montrose Press website.

CHAPTER 10

85. *White Pine Cone*, "Tomichi Topics."
86. Vandenbusche, interview with the authors.
87. Ibid.
88. Phillips, "Early Settlers."
89. Western State Colorado University. "Olympic Athletes and Coaches."
90. O'Neill, "Zip-N-Walk a Mile."
91. Strobeck, "Sagebrush Hill."
92. Ibid.
93. Ibid.
94. Fay, *Ski Tracks in the Rockies*.
95. Hollingshead, "Whitepine Ski Area."
96. Sherman, "I Forgot My Parachute."
97. *Steamboat Pilot*, "Abandoned Ski Tow."
98. MacLennan, "Pershing Ski Hill."
99. Ibid.
100. Lee, "Rozman Hill Ski Area."
101. Savage, "Marble Ski Area."
102. Nelson, *Marble & Redstone*.
103. Colorado Ski History website.
104. Schneider, "Second Mudslide Hits Marble Area."

Chapter 11

105. *Steamboat Pilot*, "News of Our Neighbors," February 24, 1938.
106. Vandenbusche, *Images of America*.
107. Fay, *Ski Tracks in the Rockies*.
108. *Aspen Daily Times*, "Hundreds Enjoy Winter Sports."
109. *Steamboat Pilot*, "News of Our Neighbors," February 24, 1938.
110. Ibid.

Chapter 12

111. Brodin, "San Isabel Ski Area Operation."
112. Walter, "Rocky Slope of Custer Skiing."
113. Bronski, *Powder Ghost Towns*, 89.
114. Ibid.
115. Brodin, "San Isabel Ski Area Operation."
116. Chamberlin, "Conquistador Ski Area."
117. Kolomitz, "Ghosts of Slopes Past."
118. *Sangre Magazine*, "Conquistador Resort."
119. Colorado Ski History website.

Chapter 13

120. Phillips, "Steady May Be the Answer."
121. Colorado Ski History website.
122. Ibid.
123. Colorado Ski Information Center, *Manual of Colorado Skiing*, 1961–62, 1963–64.
124. La Veta, Colorado website.
125. Phillips, "Steady May Be the Answer."
126. Ibid.
127. Ibid.

Chapter 14

128. Autrey, "Sugarite."
129. New Mexico Bureau of Geology and Minerals website, "Sugarite Canyon State Park."
130. Autrey, "Sugarite."

131. Ibid.
132. Heider, interview with the authors.
133. Wildermuth, "Sugarite at Turning Point."

CHAPTER 15

134. *Rocky Mountain Sun*, Item, May 10, 1884.
135. Coldville, interview with the authors.
136. Chavez, interview with the authors.

CHAPTER 16

137. Cantlin, "About Creede."
138. *Steamboat Pilot*, "Highway Workers Nearly Perish on Wolf Creek Pass."
139. *Monte Vista Journal*, "Still Skiing at 98."
140. Elliott, interview with the authors.
141. Vance, "Wolf Creek Ski Area Beginnings."
142. *Aspen Daily Times*, "Estimate 98,000 Skiers Enjoyed the Facilities."
143. Wylie, interview with the authors.
144. Birdsey, interview with the authors.

CHAPTER 17

145. *Durango-Cortez (CO) Herald*, "Coal Bank Hill Offers Skiing Rarity."
146. McDaniel, e-mail to Caryn Boddie on San Juan County, February 19, 2015.
147. Ibid.
148. *Durango Herald-Democrat*, Item, December 2, 1937.
149. Ibid., "Ski Enthusiasts Hold Meeting."
150. *Durango Herald-Democrat*, "Basin Offers Sportsman Every Thrill."
151. Miller, e-mail to Patt Emmett.
152. McDaniel, e-mail to Caryn Boddie on San Juan County, February 19, 2015.
153. Kuss, "Early-day Skiers."
154. Spencer, "Storm Peak."
155. Ibid.
156. Ibid.
157. *Durango-Cortez (CO) Herald*, "Speed Skiing."

158. Ibid.
159. Spencer, "Weber Easily Grabs Speed Skiing Championships."
160. Telluride Historical Museum video.

Chapter 18

161. *Durango Herald-Democrat*, "Basin Offers Sportsman Every Thrill."
162. McDaniel, interview with the authors.
163. Miller, e-mail to Patt Emmett.
164. McDaniel, interview with the authors.
165. Langdon, *Durango Ski*.
166. *Durango Herald-Democrat*, Item, November 23, 1947.
167. Ibid.
168. Miller, e-mail to Patt Emmett.
169. McDaniel, e-mail to Caryn Boddie on La Plata County, February 17, 2015.
170. Strode, "Snowball Effect."
171. Colorado Ski History website.
172. McMillan, "Lost Ski Areas by Name."
173. Inter-Ski Services, *White Book of US Ski Areas*, 1976.
174. *Durango-Cortez (CO) Herald*, "Tamarron to Build Ski Area."
175. Dunavant, interview with the authors.

Chapter 19

176. Ballantine, "Cortez Accomplishment." "AB, Jr., was Arthur Ballantine, Jr., who with his wife, Morley, purchased two Durango newspapers in 1952—the *Durango Herald-Democrat* and the *Durango News*—and combined them into one…the newspaper went through a number of name changes, but it has been the *Durango Herald* now for many years," wrote Robert McDaniel in a February 21, 2015 e-mail. "The Ballantine family still owns the newspaper, and Arthur and Morley's son, Richard, recently retired as publisher…Arthur always signed his editorials 'AB, Jr.' and Morley signed hers 'MCB.' The *C* in Morley's name refers to the famous newspaper family Cowles, which she was part of."
177. Allum, "Mancos Hill Ski Course."
178. Ibid.
179. Ibid.
180. Ibid.

181. *Durango Herald-News*, "Sports Roundup."

182. Ballantine, "Cortez Accomplishment."

183. Colorado Ski Information Center, *Manual of Colorado Skiing*, 1957–58.

184. Ptolemy, "Stoner Ski Area."

185. Inter-Ski Services, *White Book of US Ski Areas*, 1980, 1984.

186. Miller, e-mail to Patt Emmett.

Chapter 20

187. *Telluride Daily Journal*, Item, Weekly, March 18, 1923.

188. Telluride Historical Museum film, *We Skied It!*

189. *Telluride Daily Journal*, "Rancher Makes Trip."

190. Ibid., "Telluride Should Have Ski Club."

191. Mahoney, interview with the authors.

192. *Durango-Cortez (CO) Herald*, "Ski Dallas Expects Best Year Yet."

193. Colorado Ski History website.

Chapter 21

194. *Steamboat Pilot*, "On the Square."

195. Mahoney, interview with the authors.

196. Ibid.

197. Ouray County Historical Society photo and caption.

198. Clark, letter to Peter Boddie about Ironton Park.

199. *Durango-Cortez (CO) Herald*, "Ski Dallas Expects Best Year Yet."

Bibliography

ARTICLES

Aspen Daily Times. "Delta Ski Fans Plan Unique Party." February 12, 1924.

———. "Estimate 98,000 Skiers Enjoyed the Facilities of National Forests in Rocky Mountain Region Last Winter." May 5, 1938.

———. "Get Out Your [Skis] and Take This In." January 24, 1925.

———. "Hundreds Enjoy Winter Sports on Marshall Pass." February 17, 1938.

———. "Ski Club Sponsors Independence Pass Ski Trip." November 12, 1953.

Autrey, Pierre. "Sugarite: A Well-Kept Secret in NM." *Raton Range*, February 23, 1982.

Buena Vista Democrat. "State News." February 14, 1884.

Cantlin, James. "About Creede." Letter to Frank Lohmeister, Leadville. *Herald Democrat*, March 31, 1892.

Chamberlin, Brad. "Conquistador Ski Area: Westcliffe, Colorado, 1976–88, 1992–93." Unpublished, December 8, 2003.

Colorado Wonderland, Inc. "Skiing Centers of Colorado." *Colorado Wonderland* (Christmas 1951).

Davey, Bud. "Snow Dust." *Aspen Daily Times,* January 25, 1940.

Duffy, Neil. "Untitled." *Glenwood Post*, September 12, 1940.

Durango-Cortez (CO) Herald. "Coal Bank Hill Offers Skiing Rarity." 1966.

———. "Ski Dallas Expects Best Year Yet in Third Season of Operation." See & Ski Southwestern Colorado supplement, November 27, 1966.

———. "Speed Skiing: Storm Peak Basin above Silverton Is the Spot." March 20, 1980.

———. "Tamarron to Build Ski Area." May 24, 1981.

Durango Herald-Democrat. "Basin Offers Sportsman Every Thrill: Fishing Season Opens May 25; Big Game Hunting and Winter Sports Round Out Activities." May 13, 1951.

———. Item, November 2, 1947.

———. Item, December 2, 1937.

———. "Ski Enthusiasts Hold Meeting at Power Co. Office." November 13, 1937.

Durango Herald-News. "Sports Roundup: Week-end Skiing Outlook Rated Poor in Basin." December 31, 1958.

Eagle Valley Enterprise. "Out Door Sports Club Organized in Eagle." December 16, 1938.

———. "Ski Lift Is Near Completion." October 8, 1948.

Empire Magazine. "Colorado Ski Area Guide." November 12, 1972.

Estes Park Trail. "Colorado in Paragraphs." June 16, 1922.

Gardner-Smith, Brent. "Aspen Pioneer Roch Dies at 96." *Aspen Times*, November 21, 2002.

Glenwood Post. "Free Barbecue Will Be Oct. 26 at Red Mountain." October 16, 1941.

———. "New Ski Course Location Is Given to City." November 9, 1939.

———. "Skiing Conditions on Red Mountain Are Excellent." January 4, 1940.

Heicher, Kathy. "Skiing Eagle: Downvalley Rope Tow Ski Runs Were Years Ahead of Vail." *Eagle Valley Enterprise*, February 17, 2011.

Ignacio Chieftain. "Big Snow Storm at Ouray." October 27, 1910.

Jenkins, Mark. "A History of Skis." *National Geographic* (December 2013): 90–95.

Kawamura, Katherine. "Winter Recreation Area Operates on Mesa." *Grand Junction Daily Sentinel*, February 23, 1967.

Kirvin, David. "Jim Jackson Brings Back Speed Skiing." *Durango-Cortez Herald*, April 28, 1991.

Kolomitz, Christopher. "Ghosts of Slopes Past." *Colorado Central*. http://www.cozine.com/2012-december/ghosts-of-slopes-past.

Kuss, Dolph. "Early-day Skiers." *Historic Durango* (2001).

Monte Vista Journal. "Still Skiing at 98, Elliott in Hall of Fame." November 10, 2011. http://www.montevistajournal.com/v2_news_articles.php?story_id=2986&page=72.

Phillips, Dave. "Steady May Be the Answer." *Colorado Springs Gazette*, December 21, 2008.

Ptolemy, Andy. "Stoner Ski Area Goes Into Its 18th Season." *Durango-Cortez (CO) Herald*, November 27, 1966.

Raton Range. "Roland Chivers Injured." December 19, 1940.

Rocky Mountain Sun. Item, Aspen, CO, May 10, 1884.

Sangre Magazine (Winter 1986). "Conquistador Resort: The Place to Conquer Fun."

Savage, Vince. "Marble Ski Area: Development of Debacle?" *Marble Chips* 2 (Winter 2002–2003): 4.

Schneider, Richard J. "Second Mudslide Hits Marble Area." *Rocky Mountain News*, Tuesday, May 22, 1973.

Soncarty, Willa. "Red Mountain Helped Pioneer Western Skiing." Time and Again, *Glenwood Post*, December 27, 1998.

Spencer, Kevin. "Storm Peak Basin Groomed and Awaiting Ski Record." *Durango-Cortez (CO) Herald*, April 20, 1980.

———. "Weber Easily Grabs Speed Skiing Championships." *Durango-Cortez (CO) Herald*, April 28, 1980.

Steamboat Pilot. "Abandoned Ski Tow." October 15, 1942.

———. "Girl Makes Perilous Trip Over Divide on Skis." March 3, 1920.

———. "Highway Workers Nearly Perish on Wolf Creek Pass." December 4, 1931.

———. "New Ski School Opening at Climax." December 11, 1947.

———. "News of Our Neighbors." December 3, 1936; February 24, 1938; November 10, 1938; September 4, 1947; January 5, 1950.

———. "Northwestern Colorado: News of an Empire Condensed from Exchanges." March 11, 1925; January 6, 1928.

———. "On the Square." First item, November 17, 1938.

———. "Pagoda Woman Takes Census on Pair of Skis." March 3, 1920.

———. "Skiers Marooned in Shelter Cabin." January 14, 1937.

———. "Winter Sports in Many Sections Gaining Momentum." January 22, 1942.

Strode, Dale. "The Snowball Effect." *Durango Herald*, August 26, 2006.

Summit County Journal. "Breckenridge Should Capitalize Its Snowbanks." February 10, 1917.

———. "Local Boys Make Good Ski Records." March 11, 1922.

———. "Lower Blue River Boys Have Organized Ski Club." January 29, 1921.

———. "New Breckenridge Ski Course Ready for Big Jumpers." February 5, 1921.

———. "Ski Course Put in Fine Condition." January 7, 1922.

———. "Ski-Riding Now in Vogue." February 6, 1909.

———. "Ski Tournaments Are General Order." January 29, 1921.

———. "Why the Dillon Ski Course Is Rated as Best in the World." February 28, 1920.

Telluride Daily Journal. Item, Weekly, March 8, 1923.

———. "Rancher Makes Trip of 18 Miles on Skis." March 23, 1922.

———. "Telluride Should Have Ski Club, Says Champion Ski Jumper." April 10, 1923.

Vance, Norm. "Wolf Creek Ski Area Beginnings." *Adventure Guide*, October 13, 2010. http://pagosa.com/adventureguide/wolf-creek-ski-area-beginnings.

Walter, Hal. "The Rocky Slope of Custer Skiing." *Colorado Central Magazine* (December 1, 1996). http://cozine.com/1996-december/the-rocky-slope-of-custer-skiing.

White Pine Cone. "Tomichi Topics." January 22, 1886.

Wildermuth, Todd. "Sugarite at Turning Point; Waltons Out." *Raton Range*, June 30, 1992.

Willoughby, Tim. "Skiing Comes to Aspen: The Highland Bavarian Corporation (Part I)." *Aspen Times*, January 23, 2011.

WNU Features. "Full Flight: Winter Sports Areas Primed for Influx of Ski Enthusiasts." December 27, 1946.

Wolf, William. "K Men Ready for Cooper Hill Test." *Camp Hale Ski-Zette*, January 28, 1944.

Blog Posts and Editorials

Ballantine, Arthur, Jr. "Cortez Accomplishment." *Durango-Herald*, January 3, 1955.

Brewer, Fred. "Five More Lost Colorado Ski Areas." Colorado Skier, 1993.

Books

Bronski, Peter. *Powder Ghost Towns: Epic Backcountry Runs in Colorado's Lost Ski Resorts.* Berkeley, CA: Wilderness Press, 2008.

Coleman, Annie Gilbert. *Ski Style: Sport and Culture in the Rockies*. Lawrence: University Press of Kansas, 2004.

Dyer, John. *The Snow-Shoe Itinerant: An Autobiography*. Cincinnati, OH: Cranston & Stowe, 1891.

Fay, Abbott. *Ski Tracks in the Rockies: A Century of Colorado Skiing*. Evergreen, CO: Cordillera Press, 1984.

Gilliland, Mary Ellen. *Summit: A Gold Rush History of Summit County, Colorado*. 25th ed. Silverthorne, CO: Alpenrose Press, 2006.

Hafnor, John. *Strange but True: Weird Tales of the Wild West*. Fort Collins, CO: Lone Pine Productions, 2005.

Langdon, Charlie. *Durango Ski: People and Seasons at Purgatory*. Durango, CO: Purgatory Press, 1989.

Nelson, Jim. *Marble & Redstone: A Quick History*. 3rd ed. Glenwood Springs, CO: Blue Chicken Publishing, 2006.

Scott, Sandra. *Coincidence? I Don't Think So*. Bloomington, IN: AuthorHouse. com, 2015.

Vandenbusche, Duane. *Images of America: Around Monarch Pass*. Charleston, SC: Arcadia Publishing, 2010.

E-MAILS

Fetcher, Bill, to Caryn Boddie. August 8, 2014.

McDaniel, Robert, to Caryn Boddie. Clarifications and details, February 18, 2015.

———. Clarifications and details, October 13, 2014.

———. Clarifications and details, February 20, 2015.

———. Details about Arthur Ballantine Jr. and family, February 21, 2015.

———. La Plata County, February 17, 2015.

———. On San Juan County, February 19, 2015.

———. San Juan County, February 19, 2015.

Miller, Reese, to Patt Emmett. February 20, 2015.

BIBLIOGRAPHY

FILMS

Telluride Historical Museum. *We Skied It! Skiing in Telluride 1920's–1970's.* Documentary produced by Amy Levek and Dean Rolley, TELL Me A Story MEdia, 2009.

PAPERS AND MANUALS

Colorado Ski Information Center. *Manual of Colorado Skiing and Winter Sports 1957–58 Season : At the Top of the Nation!*
———. *Manual of Colorado Skiing and Winter Sports 1961–62 Season: At the Top of the Nation!*
———. *Manual of Colorado Skiing and Winter Sports 1962–63 Season: At the Top of the Nation!*
———. *Manual of Colorado Skiing and Winter Sports 1963–64 Season: At the Top of the Nation!*
Colorado Visitors Bureau. "Ski Area Information." Denver: Colorado Visitors Bureau, 1966.
Inter-Ski Services. *The White Book of US Ski Areas.* Washington, D.C.: Inter-Ski Services, Inc., 1965, 1976, 1980, 1984.
McMillan, John. "Lost Ski Areas by Name." N.p., April 4, 1999.
National Ski Patrol. *Ski Patrol Manual.* Denver, CO: National Ski Patrol System of America Headquarters, 1956.

PERSONAL INTERVIEWS

Birdsey, Iris. Interview with the authors. Creede, CO, August 23, 2014.
Brookshire, Joan. Interview with the authors. Leadville, CO, November 7, 2014.
Burritt, Brad. Interview by phone with Peter Boddie, February 10, 2015.
Chavez, Johnny R. Interview with the authors. Del Norte, CO, August 23, 2014.
Coldville, Louise. Interview by phone with the authors, Autumn 2014.
Dunavant, Ron. Interview with the authors. Bayfield, CO, September 26, 2014.
Elliott, Charles. Interview by phone with the authors, August 2014.

Emmett, Pat Yeager. Interview with the authors. Durango, CO, September 25, 2014.

Hayes, Mary Eshbaugh. Interview by phone with the authors, January 3, 2015.

Heider, Bret. Interview with the authors. Raton, NM, October 11, 2014.

Mahoney, Bill. Interview with the authors. Montrose, CO, October, 19, 2014.

McDaniel, Robert. Interview with the authors. Durango, CO, September 25, 2014.

Murr, Norma Lou. Interview with the authors. Walsenburg, CO, August 23, 2014.

Vandenbusche, Duane. Interview with the authors, Gunnison, CO, November 21, 2014.

Wylie, Kenny. Interview with the authors. Creede, CO, August 23, 2014.

PERSONAL REMINISCENCES

Allum, John. "Mancos Hill Ski Course (As I Remember It)." April 2007.

Brodin, George. "San Isabel Ski Area Operation." *Pueblo Lore*, August 2014.

Clark, Jack, Sr. Letter to Peter Boddie about Ironton Park, January 5, 2015.

Phillips, J.E. "Early Settlers All Used Snowshoes or Skis to Go Places." *Steamboat Pilot* (Steamboat Springs, CO), April 11, 1940.

REPORTS

Hauk, Paul. "Montezuma Basin Ski Area Chronology." Report for the USDA, Forest Service, 1978.

Hollingshead, Judith. "Whitepine Ski Area: Recreation for Miners." Thesis, Western State College, 1983.

Lee, Bob D. "Rozman Hill Ski Area: "Where's that Angel?" Thesis, Western State College, 1977.

MacLennan, Lynda K. "The Pershing Ski Hill." Thesis, Western State College, 1983.

O'Neill, Kimberly. "Zip-N-Walk a Mile: Cupola Hill." Thesis, Western State College, 1980.

Sherman, Gary J. "I Forgot My Parachute: A History of the Pioneer Ski Area." Thesis, Western State College, 1977.

Strobeck, Marilyn. "The Sagebrush Hill—Left to the Wind: The Practice Ski Course." Thesis, Western State College, 1980.

WEBSITES

Brandt, Laurie. "Cerro Summit: An Early Local Ski Area." Montrose Press. http://www.montrosepress.com/news/outdoors/cerro-summit-an-early-local-ski-area/article_3c93209e-7440-11e3-a8ee-0019bb2963f4.html.

Colorado Ski and Snowboard Museum. "1972–76 Winter Olympics." http://www.skimuseum.net/pdf/1972-76.pdf.

Colorado Ski History. http://www.coloradoskihistory.com.

La Veta, Colorado. http://www.lavetacolorado.com/uptop.html.

National Geographic. "A History of Skis." http://ngm.nationalgeographic.com/2013/12/first-skiers/ski-history-interactive.

New Mexico Bureau of Geology and Minerals. "Sugarite Canyon State Park." https://geoinfo.nmt.edu/tour/state/sugarite/home.html.

Summit Historical. "Hoosier Pass Cabin." http://www.summithistorical.org/HoosierPassCabin.html.

Summit Post. "Storm Peak." http://www.summitpost.org/storm-peak/488236.

Telluride Historical Museum. https://www.youtube.com/watch?v=tTlrbdA6Fo.

Western State Colorado University. "Olympic Athletes and Coaches from Western." http://www.western.edu/athletics/olympic-athletes-and-coaches-western.

Index

A

active community hills 20
Alexander Lake Lodge 73, 74
Allum, Jack 150
Allum, John 150, 151
Allum, Nellie 150
Alpine skiing 7, 8, 15, 20, 23, 27, 30, 128
Alta Mine 156
Alvarado 108
American Red Cross 25
American World Speed Skiing Championships 139
Animas Glacier 142
Animas Museum 132
Arapahoe Basin 30, 36, 140
Ashcroft 52, 55, 56, 58
Aspaas, Hans 142
Aspaas, Helen Ruth 142
Aspen 52, 53, 54, 55, 56, 57, 58, 60, 89, 106, 153
avalanches 162
Ayers, Bud 62

B

Bader, Clay 150
Bader, Walter 35
Balliger, Bob 132
Barnes, Jess 64
Beaver Creek 26, 44, 49
Beaver Ponds Hill 160
Benchley, Robert 55
Bergren, Bill 36, 37
B Hill 26, 44, 49, 50
Bigelow 109
bindings 16, 46, 82, 122
Birdsey, Iris 129
Black, Cole 48
Black Face 157
Boddie, Kim 103
Boomerang Road 156
Boyce, Kelly 128
Bozell, Kenny 110
Breckenridge 27, 30, 34, 35, 36
Breckenridge Ball Park 38
Breckenridge Ski Association 35
Brewer, Fred 72
Brinker, Fred 136

Brodin family 110
Brodin, George 109
Brookshire, Joan 40, 42
Broomtail Hill 160
Burrit, John and Barbara 74
Burritt, Brad 74
Buschmann, Paul 140

C

Calico Hill 145
Calkins, Bill 82
Camp Hale 26, 39, 44, 46, 49, 50, 51, 64, 113
Cantlin, James 126
Cantrell, Bruce 119
Carter Park 38
Cascade Creek 132, 135
Cascade Meadows 132, 145
Cascade Ski Courses 132, 133
Catholic Hill 156
Cedaredge 68, 72, 73, 74
Cemetery Hill 48
Cerro Summit 75
chairlifts 42
  Conquistador 112
  Doppelmayr 112
  double 146
  first chairlift in Colorado 91
  Glenwood Mountain Park 65
  Hall double 65
  Horvig 146
  Ironton Park 164
  Marble Ski Area 103
  Meadow Mountain 48
  Mesa Creek 71
  Pioneer 90, 91
  Riblet double 103
  seven-chair 164
  Sugarite 122
  Tamarron 146
  Telecar 48
Chalk Mountain 40
Chamberlin, Brad 112
Chambers, Glen 48

Chambers, Skip 46, 47
Chapman Hill 7, 20, 145
chicarica 120
Chicarica Steak House 122
Chipmunk Hill 143, 145
Civilian Conservation Corps (CCC)
    60, 61, 62, 70, 129
Clifton 68
Climax 30, 39, 40, 41, 42
Climax Mine 40
Climax Molybdenum Company 43
Cloud City Ski Club 43
Coal Bank Pass 39, 132, 136, 138
Coleman, Annie Gilbert 20
Colorado Department of Highways 128
Colorado Mountain College 43
Colorado Ski and Snowboard Hall of
    Fame 128
Colorado Ski and Snowboard Museum
    26, 36
Colorado Visitors Bureau 49, 70
Columbine Guest Ranch 145
Condotti, Joe 164
Conquistador 111, 112
Continental Divide 127
Continental Ski Club 41, 43
Continental Ski School 41
Cortez 149, 152, 153
Cowboy Hill 146
Cranor Hill 20, 87
Crawford 72
Creede Rotary Club 129
Creede Ski Hill 129
Crested Butte 78, 85, 87, 94, 95, 96, 100
Crested Butte Ski Club 93
Crystal Valley Environmental
    Protection Association 103
Cuchara 113, 114, 115, 117, 119
Cuchara Ski Basin 114, 115
Cuchara Valley 117
Culp, Russell 150
Cupola Hill 80, 81, 84, 96
Cushman Lake 160
Custer County 108, 111, 112

D

Dallas Divide 160, 164, 166
Davey, Bud 13, 75
Del Norte 124, 128, 142
Del Norte Hill 125
Delta 68, 72, 73, 79
Delta County 69, 72, 73
De Molay 43
Denver 20, 26, 37, 40, 65, 79, 103, 105, 153
De Pret, Phillippe 36, 106
Dillon 27, 29, 30, 31, 34
Dillon Reservoir 31
Dillon ski jump 34
Dole, Charles Minot 23, 25, 26
Dolores 152, 153, 157
Downey, Fred 46
downhill skiing 20, 36
Dunavant, Ron 148
Dunn, Paul 140
Durango 15, 136, 142, 143, 145, 146, 149, 150, 151
Durango & Silverton Railroad 142
Durango Ski Association 136
Durrance, Dick 58
Dutch Henry 43
Dyer, Reverend John L. 27

E

Eagle 44, 45, 46, 48, 49, 50
Eagle County 39, 44
Eagle County Historical Society 46
Eagle Ski Hill 48
Eagle Valley Winter Sports Club 45
Eccher, Joe 94
Eighty-seventh Mountain Infantry Regiment 26, 49
Elliott, Charles 128
Emmett, Patt Yeager 135, 136, 142, 143
Engineer Mountain 132, 138, 143
Erickson, Earl 150, 151
extreme skiers 22

F

Fawn Valley 73
Fetcher, Bill 21, 50
Fick, Leo 62
Finley, Les 62
Firecracker Hill 159
Fiske, Billy 53, 54, 56
Flaherty, Dick 99
Flood, Eyvind 27, 34
Flynn, R.J. 86, 87
Flynn, Tom 53, 54, 56
Fordham, Art 89
Fordham, Ellen 92, 93
Forest Lakes 147
Fort Lewis College 143
Fremont Pass 40
Fremont Trading Post 40
Front Range 13

G

Gallant, Dick 154
Galloping Goose 157
Garcia, Juan P. 123
Garfield County 60
Gilliland, Mary Ellen 30
Glenwood Mountain Park 64, 65
Glenwood Ski Club 64
Glenwood Springs 60
Goldsworthy, Ed 159
Goode, Ken 104
Gorusch, Jack 72
Grand Junction 60, 65, 68, 69, 70, 72, 74, 79, 83
Grand Junction Ski Club 69, 70
Grand Mesa 68, 69, 70, 71, 72, 73, 74
Grand Mesa Ski Carnival 68
Great Depression 83
Grizzly Gulch 156, 160
Groswold, Thor 53, 54, 92, 106
Grout, Eddie 83
Gunnison County 69, 75, 77, 79, 81, 83, 85, 86, 87, 89, 90, 93, 100, 105, 106, 107

Gunnison County Ski Club 83, 84, 87, 93, 95, 106
Gunnison Valley Ski Club. *See* Gunnison County Ski Club

H

Hafnor, John 31
Hakkinen, Kalevi 140
Harrison, Dwight 117
Haugen, Anders 29, 31, 33, 34
Haugen, Lars 29, 156
Haugen's Hill 31
Hauk, Paul 52, 57
Hayes, Mary Eshbaugh 57
Heicher, Kathy 46
Heider, Bret 122, 123
Herbert, Bernard 41
Hesperus Hill 20, 146
Hidden Valley 26
Highland Bavarian Corporation 54, 56
Highland Bavarian Lodge 55
Holiday Hill 60
Hoosier Pass 30, 36, 37
Howelsen, Carl 29
Huerfano County 114, 117

I

Independence Pass 52
International Olympic Committee (IOC) 26
International Speed Skiing Association 140
Ironton Park 163, 164
Irwin 78

J

Jackson, Jim 140, 141
Jarvis Meadows 132, 135
Jencks, Moses Amos 85
Johnson, Bill 48
Jones, Ed 64
Juhan, Joe 64

K

Kauffman, James 42
Kendall Mountain 7, 20
Keystone 36
Kidder, Barbara 92
Kirkendall, W.E. 65
Kistler, Frank 58
Knowles, John 82
Krizmanich, Steve 94
Kullerstand, Ralph 164
Kuss, Adolph 83, 96, 143

L

Lake City Ski Hill 20
Lake County 39
Lake, Henry F. 81, 84
Lake, Rial 81, 83, 89, 90, 106
Lands End 68, 69
Langes, Gunther 55
La Plata County 132, 142, 143
Las Animas County 120
Leadville 26, 39, 40, 43, 50, 51
Lead-Zinc 86
Lechner Field 143
Lee, Jack 133, 145
Lee's Ski Slope 20
Lenihan, B.J. 140
Lime Creek Road 132
Lions Club 48
Little Annie Basin 52, 53, 54, 55
Little Sweden Freezer Company 36
Lizard Head Pass 157, 160, 164
Locarnini, Margaret 113
Longfellow, Livingston 25
Lookout Mountain 61
Loveland Pass 30, 36
Lovett, Emory 150

M

Magnussen, Anne Marie 33
Mahoney, Bill "Senior" 155, 157, 159, 162, 164
Mahoney, Bob 157, 159, 160
mail carriers 27, 77, 166
Mammoth Slide 157
Mancos Hill Ski Club 150, 151

Mancos Hill Ski Course 149
Marble 100, 102, 103
Marble Ski Area 80, 100, 101
Marolt, Max 58
Marshall Pass 79, 105, 106, 107
Martin-Kuntz, Marti 140
McClure, Bill 64
McClure, Randy 130
McDaniel, Robert 132, 136, 142, 143,
    145, 146, 152
McDermott, Wes 90, 106
McEnhill, Ray 112
McKinney, Steve 140
McLean, Barney 92
McMillan, Jerry 99
McMillan, John 146
Meadow Mountain 48, 49
Means, George 86, 87
Mesa County 68
Mesa Creek 68, 69, 70
Mesa Lakes 68, 69
Mesa Nature and Sports Club. *See*
    Grand Junction Ski Club
Mill Creek 132, 136, 149
Mill Creek Lodge 131, 136, 138
Miller, Audrey 90
Miller, Bob 140
Miller, Leo 35
Miller, Reese 15, 22, 136, 143, 145, 154
Million Dollar Highway 132
Milstein, Dick 58, 112
Mineral County 126, 128
Mines and Memories 129
mining 30, 39, 43, 55, 58, 86, 87, 90, 93,
    120, 124, 126, 136, 155, 157, 162
Montezuma Basin 52, 56, 57, 58
Montezuma County 149
Montrose County 75, 79
Mountaineers 80, 96
Murr, Floyd 115
Murr, Norma Lou 114, 115, 117

N

National Forest Foundation 26
National Park Service 62

National Ski Patrol. *See* ski patrol
night skiing 40, 42, 43, 83, 84, 122,
    146, 161
Nordic skiing 15, 23, 27
Norway 27, 33
Norwegian snowshoes 13, 52, 77, 142

O

Oberlander Corporation 103
Old La Veta Pass 115
Olympics 8, 13, 16, 26, 33, 34, 49, 77, 80
    1924 Winter Games 31
    1976 Winter Games 26, 143
Ouray County 17, 162, 163, 164

P

Palmer, Bruce 157
Panadero 117
Paonia 73
Peak 1 31
Perry-Smith, Crosby 80, 95
Pershing Ski Hill 93, 96
Pioneer 84, 86, 87, 89, 90, 92, 93, 94, 95
Pitkin County 52
Poma lifts 122, 123
    Forest Lakes 147
    Meadow Mountain 48
    Mesa Creek 70
    Sugarite 122
Porcupine Gulch 36
powder 13, 122, 137, 138
Powderhorn Ski Area 68, 69, 70, 71
Prestrud Jump 31
Prestrud, Peter 27, 31
Prospect Basin 156
Purgatory 136, 146, 147

Q

Quick's Hill 84, 85

R

rancher 15, 46, 66, 97, 112, 123, 155, 166
Randall, Eileen 46
Randall, Florence 46

Randall, Mick 46, 47
Raton 120, 122, 123
Raton Basin Ski Area 120
Red Cliff 26, 50
Redlands Mesa 74
Red Mountain 60, 61, 63, 64, 65
Redstone 52, 58, 59
Redstone Development Company 58
Rees, Claude 66
Rees Ski Ranch 66, 67
Reida, Clara 113
Richardson, Norman 41
Rico 157
Ridgway 160, 162
Rifle Ski Club 66
Rimrock 73, 74
Rimrock Winter Sports Area 74
Rio Blanco County 66, 67
Rio Grande and Southern Railroad 157
Rio Grande County 105, 124
risk 22, 23
Rist, Louis 133
Roberts, Milton 150
Roch, Andre 55, 56
Roch Run 56, 75
Rockwell, Clarence 84
rope tows 30, 42
  Breckenridge Ball Park 38
  Cedaredge 73
  Cerro Summit 76
  Columbine Guest Ranch 145
  Cowboy Hill 146
  Creede Ski Hill 129
  Cupola Hill 83
  Dallas Divide 164
  Del Norte Hill 125
  Eagle Ski Hill 48
  Fawn Valley 73
  Firecracker Hill 159
  Grizzly Gulch 160
  Holiday Hills 60
  Hoosier Pass 36
  Lizard Head Pass 157
  Mancos Hill 150
  Mesa Creek 70

Montezuma Basin 56, 57
Pershing Ski Hill 94
Pioneer 90
Porcupine Gulch 36
Rees Ski Ranch 67
Rimrock 74
Rozman Hill 96
Sagebrush Hills 84
Silver Hills 113
Ski San Isabel 109
Skyline Ranch 160
Stoner 153
Sugarite 122
Tamarron 146
Telluride Beaver Ponds 160
Top O' La Veta 117
Whittaker Hill 45
Whittaker Ranch 46
Wolf Creek Pass 128
Rosen, Richard 57
Rotary Club 75, 129
Rowan, Robert 53, 54
Royal Mountain 31
Rozman Hill 93, 94, 95, 96, 98,
  99, 100
Rozman, John 95, 97, 98
Ryan, Ted 53, 54, 55, 56

S

Sagebrush Hill 66, 83
Saguache County 105
Sams 160
Sands, Guy 160
San Juan Basin 142
San Juan Basin Ski and Winter Sports
  Association 133
San Juan County 131, 132, 142, 145
San Juan Mountains 124, 138, 162
San Juan Ski Club 162
San Luis Valley 124, 127, 128
San Luis Valley Ski Association 128
San Miguel County 155, 164
Sargents 77, 86
Saya, Joe 94
Schaeffler, Willy 58

Schneibs, Otto 54
Schweitzer, Charles 106
Scott, Sandra 73
Shaikily, Mund 112
Shock Hill 27, 34, 35
Silver Cliff 108
Silver Hills 113
Silverton 132, 136, 138, 139, 140, 141, 142, 162
Silverton Chamber of Commerce 140
Singing Acres Ranch 113
sitzmarks 151
ski bike 46, 47
Ski Cooper 26, 39, 43, 50
Ski Dallas 160, 161, 164, 166
Ski-Hi Ski Club 152, 153, 154
ski jumping 15, 23, 27, 31, 34, 35, 69
ski patrol 13, 22, 24, 25, 26, 40, 49, 64, 65, 67, 70, 71, 74, 125, 128, 153
skis
  Anderson 16
  Northland 16, 82
  Thompson 16
Ski San Isabel 109
Skyline Guest Ranch 160
Skyline Ranch 160
Slate Creek 35
Slate Creek Ski Club 35
Small Business Administration 110, 112
Smith, Margaret "Cap" 64
snowfall 21, 58, 59, 63, 64, 68, 146
snowmaking 43, 112, 122, 146
Somerset 73
Somrak, John 94
South Fork 124, 157
South Park Lions Club 36
Spencer, Kevin 138, 139, 140
Steamboat Springs 26, 64, 69, 156
Steele, Charles 129
Steinbeck, Anne 86, 87
Stoner 149, 152, 153, 154
Storm Peak Basin 138, 140
Storm Peak, Inc. 140

Stroud, Howard 102
Stump, Alain 140
Sugarite 120, 123
Summit County 17, 27, 29, 30, 34
Summitville 124
Sunlight Mountain Resort and Ski Area 60
Sweitzer, Chuck 89

T

Tagert, Billy 55
Tagert ranch 55
Tamarron 140, 146, 147
Taos Ski Valley Resort 117
T-bar lifts 40, 42, 59, 152, 153, 154, 161
  Dallas Divide 166
  Redstone 58
  Ski Dallas 161
  Stoner 152
Telluride Historical Museum 140, 155
Telluride Ski Club 157
Tenmile Range 31
Tenth Mountain Division 13, 25, 26, 30, 39, 41, 44, 49, 56, 164
Texas 117, 118, 153
Third Avenue Hill 145
Thornton, Tony 160
Tombling, Clarence 91
Top O' La Veta 115
tournaments 35, 69, 155, 156
Trujillo, Juan Antonio 115
Trumbull, Joan 93
Turkey Creek Mesa 160
Turner, Nick 145

U

Union Carbide 67
Up Top 115
U.S. Forest Service (USFS) 20, 49, 52, 54, 56, 58, 70, 83, 89, 90, 91, 96, 103, 117, 119, 129, 133, 138, 150, 151

V

Vail 26, 36, 48, 49
Vandenbusche, Duane 77, 86
Velocity Peak 138, 141

W

Walton, LaBelle and Millard 121
Walton, Lynette 123
Walton, Millard and LaBelle 120
Walton, Robert and Ruth 120
Weber, Franz 140
Westcliffe 108, 111, 113
Western State College Hiking and
      Outing Club 84
Western State College (WSC) 80, 83,
      93, 94, 95, 96, 98
Western State Colorado University
      (WSCU) 11, 77, 80, 81
Wet Mountain Valley 108
Whitepine 86, 87, 93
Whittaker, Gordon 46
Whittaker Hill 45, 46, 47
Whittaker, LaVeta 44, 46
Whittaker Ranch 44
Whitttaker, Gordon 44
Wiik, Sven 83, 94, 95, 96, 97, 98
Wince, George 129
Wolf Creek Pass 125, 127, 128
Works Progress Administration (WPA)
      83, 84, 90
World War II 25, 36, 37, 45, 63, 73,
      80, 83, 86, 92, 94, 95, 113, 114,
      115, 130, 145
WSC ski team 93, 94
Wylie, Kenny 129

Y

Yeager family 135, 136, 143
Yeager Ranch 146

Z

Zugelder, Ann 81

About the Authors

Caryn and Peter Boddie have been skiing since childhood and enjoying Colorado for years. Caryn learned to ski at Loveland and Vail. Peter learned to ski in Connecticut. Previously, they authored *Lost Ski Areas of Colorado's Front Range and Northern Mountains* for The History Press. They

Authors Peter and Caryn Boddie ride the shuttle back to their car with a young friend after a day of skiing at Sunlight Mountain.

also created *The Hiker's Guide to Colorado*, *Hiking Colorado I* and *Hiking Colorado II*, which took them down hundreds of miles of trails. They still love traveling the state and talking to people. Peter works as a hydrologist and is the geographer of the team. Caryn is a writer and editor and works in communications. They live in South Jefferson County.